Block Buster QUILTS

I Love House Blocks

14 Quilts from an All-Time Favorite Block

Compiled by Karen M. Burns

Martingale®
Create with Confidence

Block-Buster Quilts
I Love House Blocks: 14 Quilts from an All-Time Favorite Block
© 2017 by Martingale & Company®

Martingale®
19021 120th Ave. NE, Ste. 102
Bothell, WA 98011-9511 USA
ShopMartingale.com

Printed in China
22 21 20 19 18 17   8 7 6 5 4 3 2 1

Library of Congress Cataloging-in-Publication Data
is available upon request.

ISBN: 978-1-60468-858-0

MISSION STATEMENT

We empower makers who use fabric and yarn to make life more enjoyable.

CREDITS

PUBLISHER AND
CHIEF VISIONARY OFFICER
Jennifer Erbe Keltner

CONTENT DIRECTOR
Karen Costello Soltys

DESIGN MANAGER
Adrienne Smitke

MANAGING EDITOR
Tina Cook

COVER AND
INTERIOR DESIGNER
Regina Girard

ACQUISITIONS EDITOR
Karen M. Burns

PHOTOGRAPHER
Brent Kane

TECHNICAL EDITOR
Beth Bradley

ILLUSTRATOR
Sandy Huffaker

COPY EDITOR
Durby Peterson

Contents

Introduction

Home is where the heart is. It takes hands to build a house, but only hearts build a home. A loving heart makes a happy home.

There seems to be no shortage of colloquialisms when it comes to home. Is it any wonder then that quilters have embraced House blocks for generations? I think not. After all, having a quilt-filled home is one of the comforts we embrace as quiltmakers. With that in mind, we're paying homage to the House block as a classic favorite in this fourth book in the Blockbuster Quilts series.

But just as the word *home* conjures different images in our minds, so too does the image of a House block conjure different interpretations among the designers who make them. For some, it's a traditional house with one door, two windows, and a chimney. For others, it's a tall and slender brownstone. Still others evoke memories of the "houses" we built as kids from rectangular blocks with triangle roofs. Whatever comes to mind for you, you're sure to find one (or more) that suits your style when you peruse the 14 House block quilt patterns that fill these pages.

I think William Shakespeare was nearly spot-on when he wrote, "People are usually happiest at home" quilting. (I added that last word! Don't you agree?)

Happy house building!

Jennifer Keltner,
Publisher and Chief Visionary Officer

House Blocks 101

Houses in quilt blocks come in many shapes and forms, from a simple cottage with a peaked roof to an elegant mansion with lots of windows and chimneys. No matter the size or complexity, a House block is a familiar symbol of home, adding a touch of comfort and warmth to a quilt. Despite the countless variations among House blocks, most of them share the same elements—a base topped by a roof. The base is usually a square or rectangle, and the roof is usually a triangle or trapezoid. Read on to learn how to make two simple House blocks, including easy techniques that you can apply to create triangular or trapezoid shapes for any block.

Flying-Geese Roof

The following instructions are for a 6½" × 7½" block, including the seam allowances. The triangular roof is made from one flying-geese unit. Use the method below to make one flying-geese unit at a time. Refer to "Fantastic Four" on page 8 to learn a method for making four units at once.

Select one fabric for the background (A), one fabric for the roof and door (B), and one fabric for the base (C).

1. Cut the shapes needed:
   Fabric A:
   > 2 squares, 3½" × 3½"

   Fabric B:
   > 1 rectangle, 3½" × 6½"
   > 1 rectangle, 2½" × 3½"

   Fabric C:
   > 2 rectangles, 2½" × 4½"
   > 1 rectangle, 1½" × 2½"

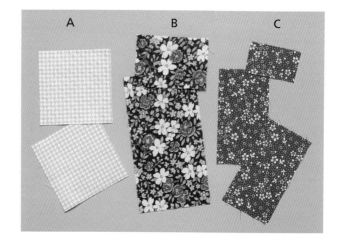

2. Draw a diagonal line from corner to corner on the wrong side of the A squares. Place one marked A square on one end of the large B rectangle with right sides together, orienting the drawn line as shown. Sew on the drawn line.

Mark.

Sew.

3. Trim the seam allowances to ¼". Press the square away from the rectangle.

Cut.

Press.

4. Place a second marked square on the opposite end of the rectangle, orienting the line as shown. Sew on the line; then trim and press the square in the same manner as the first square. There should be ¼" of seam allowance above the point of the fabric B triangle. The flying-geese unit is complete.

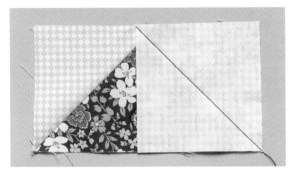

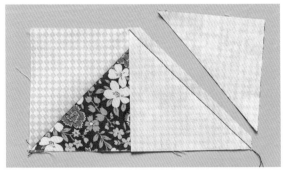

¼" seam allowance

When you need to make rooftops for a lot of blocks, this method comes in handy because it yields four flying-geese units at once. To calculate the size of the pieces to cut, use these formulas:

❖ Size to cut large square = desired finished *width* of flying geese + 1¼". For a finished 3" × 6" unit, the large square should be 7¼".

❖ Size to cut small squares = desired finished *height* of flying geese + ⅞". For a finished 3" × 6" unit, the small squares should be 3⅞".

1. Cut one large square and four small squares according to the formulas above. Draw a diagonal line from corner to corner on the wrong side of each of the four small squares. Place two small squares on opposite corners of the large square with right sides together as shown. The corners of the small squares will overlap slightly and the drawn line should extend across the large square from corner to corner. Sew ¼" from both sides of the drawn line.

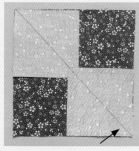
Mark.

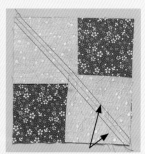
Sew on both sides of the line.

2. Cut along the drawn line, and then press the seam allowances toward the small triangles.

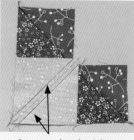
Cut.

Press.

3. Place a marked square on the corner of each unit from step 2 with right sides together, orienting the line as shown from the corner to the point between the two triangles. Sew ¼" from both sides of the marked line.

Mark.

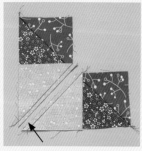
Sew on both sides of the line.

4. Cut along each drawn line, yielding two units each for a total of four units. Press the seam allowances toward the small triangles.

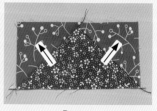
Cut.

Press.

5. Sew the small C rectangle to one end of the small B rectangle. Press the seam allowances toward B. Sew the pieced unit between the two large fabric C rectangles. Press the seam allowances toward C.

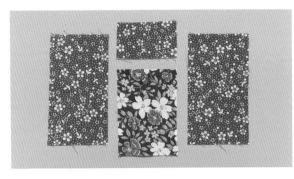

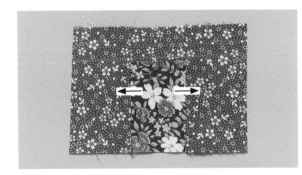

6. Sew the flying-geese unit to the top of the completed base. Press the seam allowances toward the base.

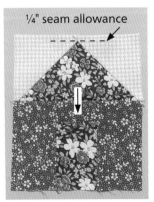

¼" seam allowance

Trapezoid Roof

The following instructions are for a 6½" × 7½" block, including the seam allowances. The roof is made from a 2½" × 6½" trapezoid unit. Select one fabric for the background (A), one fabric for the roof and door (B), and one fabric for the base (C).

1. Cut the shapes needed:
Fabric A:
  2 squares, 2½" × 2½"
Fabric B:
  1 rectangle, 2½" × 6½"
  1 rectangle, 2½" × 3½"
Fabric C:
  2 rectangles, 2½" × 5½"
  1 square, 2½" × 2½"

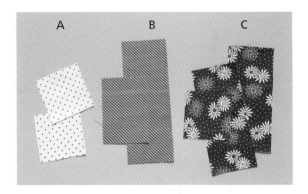

2. Draw a diagonal line from corner to corner on the wrong side of the A squares. Place one marked A square on one end of the large B rectangle with right sides together, orienting the drawn line as shown. Sew on the line.

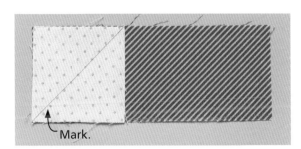
Mark.

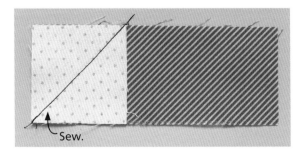
Sew.

3. Trim the seam allowances to ¼". Press the corner fabric away from the rectangle.

Cut.

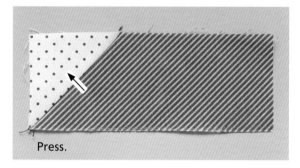
Press.

4. Place a second marked square on the opposite end of the rectangle, orienting the line as shown. Sew on the line, and then trim and press the square in the same manner as the first square. The trapezoid unit is complete.

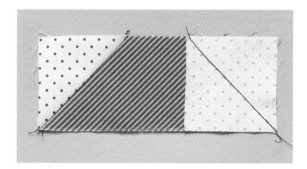

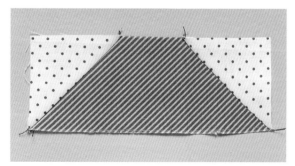

5. Sew the C square to one end of the small B rectangle. Press the seam allowances toward B. Sew the pieced unit between the two fabric C rectangles. Press the seam allowances toward C.

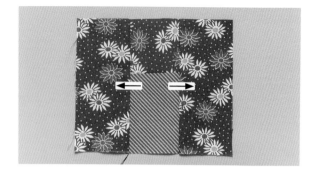

6. Sew the trapezoid unit to the top of the completed base. Press the seam allowances toward the base.

Equilateral Triangles

Another common roof shape for House blocks is an equilateral triangle. An equilateral triangle, also called a 60° triangle, has three sides of equal length and requires a different process to construct than a flying-geese unit. Follow these steps to cut and construct an equilateral-triangle roof. Choose one fabric for the roof (A) and one for the background (B).

1. If you don't have a special ruler designed for cutting equilateral triangles, use the 60° line on your quilting ruler. Cut a strip of fabric A according to the desired *height* of the triangle (not the length of the edges). To determine this measurement, add ¾" to the finished size of the triangle. For example, for a finished 3"-tall triangle, cut a 3¾"-wide strip. Place the 60° line of the ruler along the long edge of the strip, and then cut along the edge of the ruler.

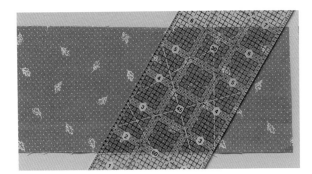

2. Align the 60° mark with the opposite side of the strip, and then cut along the edge of the ruler to make a triangle.

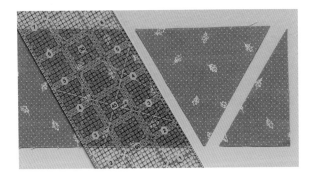

3. To make the background pieces, cut a 3¾"-wide strip from fabric B. With the strip folded in half (right or wrong sides together, it doesn't matter), place the 60° line of the ruler along the long edge of the fabric and cut along the edge of the ruler. Discard the trimmed piece.

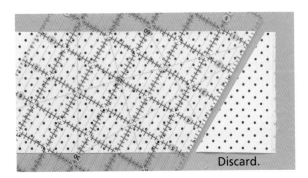

Discard.

4. With the ruler perpendicular to the long edge of the fabric, measure over ¼" from the first cut and cut across the fabric. You now have mirror image triangles for the two sides of the roof. Continue cutting in this way, making sure to leave a ¼" width at the narrow end of the triangles as you go.

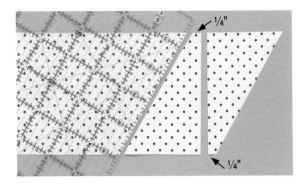

¼"

¼"

5. Place the left B triangle on the left edge of the A triangle, right sides together. Join, and then press the B triangle away from the A triangle.

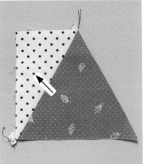

6. Sew the right B triangle to the right edge of the A triangle, and then press. There should be ¼" of B fabric above the top point of the A triangle to account for the seam allowance. Square up and trim the edges of the unit.

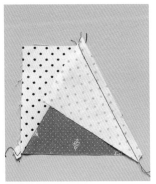

¼" seam allowance

Sherbet Town

Solid fabrics in sherbet tones make for a sweet and cheerful neighborhood. Frame each simple House block with a coordinating double border for a pleasing finished look.

Materials

Yardage is based on 42"-wide fabric.

⅓ yard *each* of 1 dark and 1 light shade of 8 assorted pastel solids (16 shades total) for blocks and binding: green, pink, blue, taupe, orange, coral, mint, and yellow

1½ yards of white solid for background

1½ yards of cream solid for sashing

5 yards of fabric for backing

83" × 83" square of batting

Cutting

All measurements include ¼" seam allowances.

From *each* of the 16 assorted pastel solids, cut:

❖ 1 strip, 2½" × 42"; crosscut into 3 rectangles, 2½" × 12½"
❖ 1 strip, 2½" × 42"; crosscut into 4 rectangles, 2½" × 8½"
❖ 1 strip, 4½" × 42"; crosscut into:
    1 rectangle, 4½" × 8½"
    1 rectangle, 2½" × 12½"
    1 rectangle, 2½" × 3"
    1 rectangle, 2" × 5½"
    2 rectangles, 2" × 3"

From the remainder of *8* of the pastel solids, cut:

❖ 1 strip, 2½" × 42", for scrappy binding

From the white solid, cut:

❖ 4 strips, 4½" × 42"; crosscut into 32 squares, 4½" × 4½"
❖ 2 strips, 4½" × 42"; crosscut into 32 rectangles, 2" × 4½"
❖ 10 strips, 2½" × 42"; crosscut into 153 squares, 2½" × 2½"

From the cream solid, cut:

❖ 20 strips, 2½" × 42"; crosscut into 40 rectangles, 2½" × 16½"

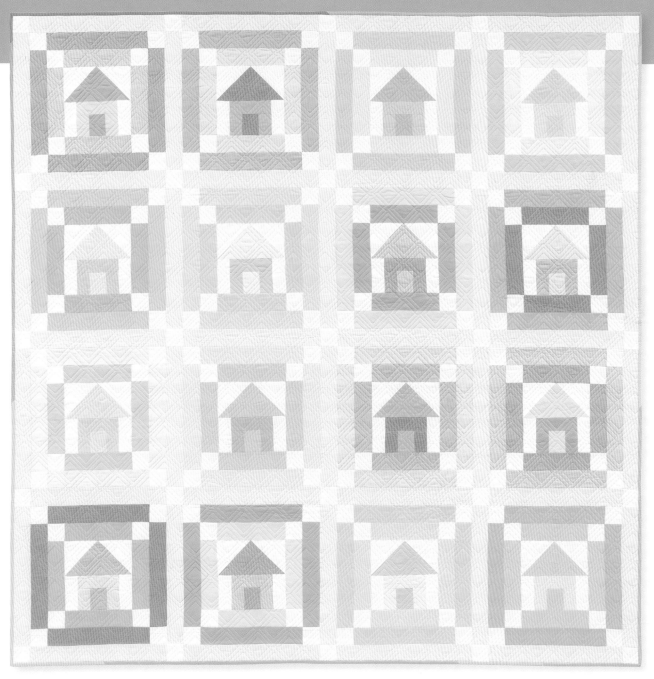

Sherbet Town by Corey Yoder; quilted by Kaylene Parry
FINISHED QUILT: 74½" × 74½"
FINISHED BLOCK: 16" × 16"

Making the House Blocks

The quilt contains 16 House blocks: two made from each of the eight colors. Pair the light and dark shades of each color to make a pair of blocks—for example, the light green house has a dark green door and roof, and vice versa.

Press all seam allowances in the directions indicated by the arrows.

1. Draw a diagonal line from corner to corner on the wrong side of the white 4½" squares. Place a marked square on one end of a dark green 4½" × 8½" rectangle with right sides together. Sew on the drawn line, and then trim ¼" from the seam. Press.

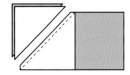

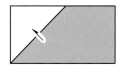

Make 16 units,
4½" × 8½".

2. Place a second white square on the opposite end of the rectangle, and then sew, trim, and press. This flying-geese unit is the roof section of the block. Repeat to make one roof from each solid for a total of 16 units. The units should measure 4½" × 8½", including the seam allowances.

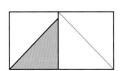
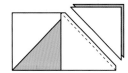

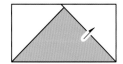

Make 16 units,
4½" × 8½".

3. Sew a light green 2" × 3" rectangle to each long side of the dark green 2½" × 3" rectangle. The unit should measure 3" × 5½". Sew a light green 2" × 5½" rectangle to the top of the unit. The unit should measure 4½" × 5½", including the seam allowances.

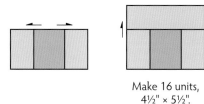

Make 16 units,
4½" × 5½".

4. Sew white 2" × 4½" rectangles to the sides of the unit, which should now measure 4½" × 8½". Sew the dark green roof to the top of the unit to complete the house. Make 16 blocks (two from each color pairing). The blocks should measure 8½" square, including the seam allowances.

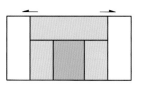

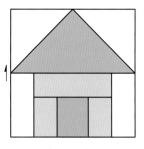

Make 16 blocks,
8½" × 8½".

Adding the Borders

Pair each of the House block colors with borders from a different color family. The four pairings Corey chose are green/pink, blue/taupe, orange/coral, and mint/yellow. If the house has a light roof, use the dark shade for the inner border. If the house has a dark roof, use the light shade for the inner border. For example, for the house with the dark green roof, the inner border is light pink. For the house with the light green roof, the inner border is dark pink.

1. Sew light pink 2½" × 8½" rectangles to opposite sides of the House block with the dark green roof. The unit should measure 8½" × 12½", including the seam allowances.

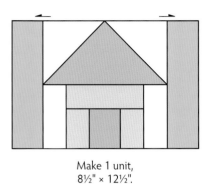

Make 1 unit,
8½" × 12½".

2. Sew a white 2½" square to each end of a light pink 2½" × 8½" rectangle. Repeat to make two pieced units that measure 2½" × 12½".

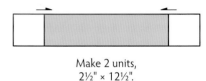

Make 2 units,
2½" × 12½".

3. Sew the units to the top and bottom of the block. The unit should measure 12½" square, including the seam allowances.

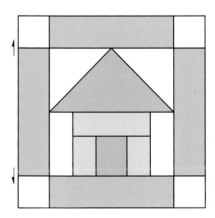

Make 1 unit,
12½" × 12½".

4. Sew dark pink 2½" × 12½" rectangles to opposite sides of the block. The unit should measure 12½" × 16½", including the seam allowances.

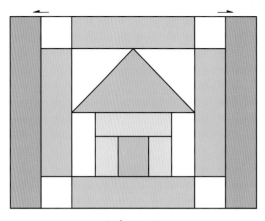

Make 1 unit,
12½" × 16½".

5. Sew a white 2½" square to each end of a dark pink 2½" × 12½" rectangle. Repeat to make two pieced units that measure 2½" × 16½".

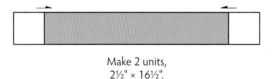

Make 2 units,
2½" × 16½".

6. Sew the units to the top and bottom of the block. The block should measure 16½" square, including the seam allowances.

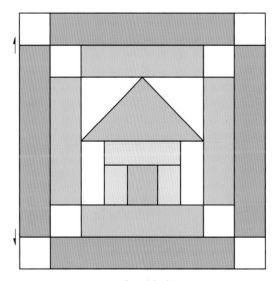

Make 1 block,
16½" × 16½".

7. Repeat steps 1–6 to make four blocks from each color pairing for a total of 16 blocks. For example, the pink/green color pairing yields four blocks as shown.

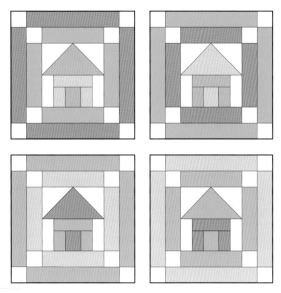

Each color pairing
will yield 4 blocks.

Assembling the Quilt Top

The quilt contains four block rows alternating with five sashing rows as shown in the quilt assembly diagram. For each block row, lay out four blocks alternating with five cream 2½" × 16½" strips. For each sashing row, lay out four cream 2½" × 16½" strips alternating with five white 2½" squares. Join the units in each row, and then join the rows.

Finishing the Quilt

Go to ShopMartingale.com/HowtoQuilt for more details on quilting and finishing.

1. Layer the backing, batting, and quilt top; baste the layers together. Hand or machine quilt as desired. The quilt shown was machine quilted with an allover diagonal grid of squares.

2. Use the assorted pastel 2½"-wide strips to make scrappy binding and then attach it to the quilt.

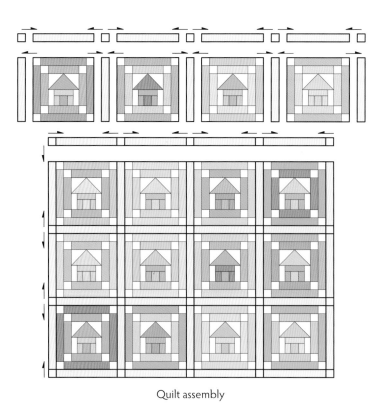

Quilt assembly

Block Party

Materials

Yardage is based on 42"-wide fabric.

1⅜ yards *total* of assorted prints for houses and roofs: aqua, pink, and red

¼ yard of white dot for windows and doors

¼ yard of blue print for chimneys and window accents

2⅛ yards of white solid for background

⅜ yard *total* of assorted green prints for trees

⅛ yard of brown tone on tone for tree trunks

½ yard of red dot for pinwheels

¾ yard of aqua dot for sashing

1⅛ yards of white floral for border

¾ yard of red-and-pink stripe for binding

4⅜ yards of fabric for backing

74" × 78" piece of batting

Cutting

All measurements include ¼" seam allowances. This quilt contains 9 House blocks, 6 Tree blocks, and 18 Pinwheel blocks. Cutting for each group of blocks is given separately below.

1 HOUSE BLOCK

For each House block, select one of the assorted aqua, pink, or red prints for the house and a contrasting aqua, pink, or red print for the roof. Determine the desired house/roof color pairings for the 9 House blocks and organize the following pieces into those groupings before cutting the fabric. Repeat the cutting instructions below for a total of 9 House blocks.

From the roof print, cut:

❖ 1 rectangle, 5" × 12½"

Continued on page 19

Create a community of happy homes and green trees in this fun-to-make row quilt. Use a scrappy assortment of bright prints to give each House block its own color scheme and character.

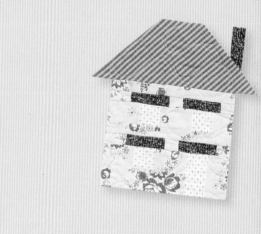

Block Party by Sherri Falls
FINISHED QUILT: 65½" × 70"
FINISHED HOUSE BLOCK: 13½" × 15"

Continued from page 17

From the house print, cut:

- ❖ 1 strip, 2" × 42"; crosscut into:
  1 rectangle, 2" × 6½"
  4 rectangles, 2" × 2¾"
  1 rectangle, 2" × 3½"
  1 square, 2" × 2"
- ❖ 1 strip, 1¼" × 42"; crosscut into:
  2 rectangles, 1¼" × 9½"
  2 rectangles, 1¼" × 2"
  4 rectangles, 1¼" × 1½"

From the white dot, cut:

- ❖ 1 rectangle, 2" × 3½"
- ❖ 3 squares, 2" × 2"

From the blue print, cut:

- ❖ 1 rectangle, 1½" × 5"
- ❖ 4 rectangles, 1¼" × 3¼"

From the white solid, cut:

- ❖ 1 rectangle, 5" × 9"; crosscut into:
  1 square, 5" × 5"
  1 rectangle, 2½" × 5"
- ❖ 2 strips, 2" × 42"; crosscut into:
  2 rectangles, 2" × 14"
  1 rectangle, 2" × 12½"
  2 rectangles, 2" × 8"
  1 rectangle, 2" × 5"

TREE BLOCKS

From the white solid, cut:

- ❖ 1 strip, 3¼" × 42"; crosscut into 6 rectangles,
  3¼" × 5"
- ❖ 2 strips, 2¼" × 42"; crosscut into 12 rectangles,
  2¼" × 3¼"
- ❖ 2 strips, 2" × 42"; crosscut into 24 squares,
  2" × 2"
- ❖ 1 strip, 1½" × 42"; crosscut into 24 squares,
  1½" × 1½"

From the green prints, cut:

- ❖ 6 matching pairs of 2 rectangles, 4¼" × 5"
  (12 total)

From the brown tone on tone, cut:

- ❖ 6 rectangles, 1½" × 3¼"

PINWHEELS

From the white solid, cut:

- ❖ 15 strips, 2" × 42"; crosscut into:
  72 rectangles, 2" × 3½"
  144 squares, 2" × 2"

From the red dot, cut:

- ❖ 7 strips, 2" × 42"; crosscut into 72 rectangles,
  2" × 3½"

SASHING, BORDERS, AND BINDING

From the aqua dot, cut:

- ❖ 12 strips, 2" × 42"

From the white floral, cut:

- ❖ 8 strips, 4½" × 42"

From the red-and-pink stripe, cut:

- ❖ 8 strips, 2½" × 42"

Making the House Blocks

Press all seam allowances in the directions indicated by the arrows.

1. Draw a diagonal line from corner to corner on the wrong side of one white solid 5" square. Place the square on the left end of a 5" × 12½" roof rectangle, right sides together, orienting the drawn line as shown. Stitch along the line, and then trim the seam allowances to ¼". Press.

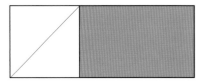

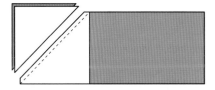

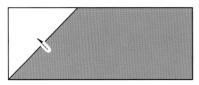

Make 1 unit,
5" × 12½".

2. To assemble the chimney unit, sew a white solid 2" × 5" rectangle to the left side of a blue 1½" × 5" rectangle. Sew a white solid 2½" × 5" rectangle to the right side of the blue rectangle. The chimney unit should measure 5" square, including the seam allowances.

Make 1 unit,
5" × 5".

3. Place the chimney unit on the opposite end of the roof unit, right sides together, orienting the segments of the chimney unit horizontally as shown. Make sure the 2"-wide white segment is on the bottom. Mark and sew diagonally from corner to corner across the chimney unit in the same manner as for the white 5" square from step 1. Trim the seam allowances to ¼"; press. The roof unit should measure 5" × 12½", including the seam allowances.

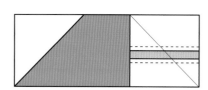

Make 1 unit,
5" × 12½".

4. Gather the matching pieces for the house section that coordinates with the roof unit just assembled. Lay out the house 1¼" × 2" rectangle and two house 1¼" × 1½" rectangles alternating with two blue 1¼" × 3¼" rectangles as shown. Make sure to place the house 1¼" × 2" rectangle on the left. Join the units along the short edges. Make two. The units should measure 1¼" × 9½", including the seam allowances.

Make 2 units,
1¼" × 9½".

5. Lay out two house 2" × 2¾" rectangles and one house 2" square alternating with two white dot 2" squares as shown, making sure to place the house 2" square on the right. Join the pieces along the short edges. The unit should measure 2" × 9½", including the seam allowances.

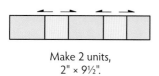

Make 2 units,
2" × 9½".

6. Sew two house 2" × 2¾" rectangles to the sides of one white dot 2" square. The pieced unit should measure 2" × 6½", including the seam allowances. Sew one house 2" × 6½" rectangle to the bottom of the pieced unit. The unit should measure 3½" × 6½", including the seam allowances.

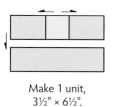

Make 1 unit,
3½" × 6½".

7. Sew a white dot 2" × 3½" rectangle to a house 2" × 3½" rectangle. The unit should measure 3½" square, including the seam allowances.

Make 1 unit,
3½" × 3½".

8. Join the left edge of the unit from step 7 to the right edge of the unit from step 6. The unit should measure 3½" × 9½", including the seam allowances.

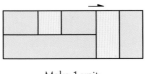

Make 1 unit,
3½" × 9½".

9. To assemble the house section of the block, lay out the two house 1¼" × 9½" rectangles, the two units from step 4, and the units from steps 5 and 8 as shown. Join the units along the long edges to make a pieced unit that measures 8" × 9½". Sew two white solid 2" × 8" rectangles to the sides of the unit to make a house section that measures 8" × 12½", including the seam allowances.

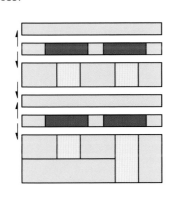

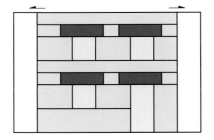

Make 1 unit,
8" × 12½".

10. Sew the roof section to the top of the house section. The completed house unit should measure 12½" square. Sew a white solid 2" × 12½" rectangle to the top of the block; press. Sew the white solid 2" × 14" rectangles to the sides of the block. Repeat steps 1–10 to make a total of nine House blocks. The finished House blocks should measure 15½" × 14", including the seam allowances.

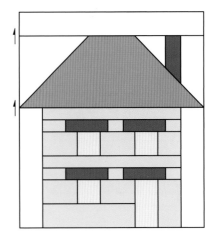

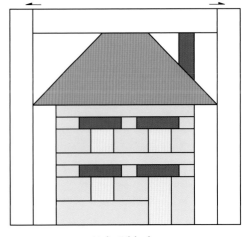

Make 9 blocks,
15½" × 14".

Making the Tree Blocks

1. Draw a diagonal line from corner to corner on the wrong side of four white solid 2" squares and four white solid 1½" squares. Select a matching pair of green rectangles. Place 2" marked squares on the upper corners of one green rectangle and 1½" squares on the lower corners as shown on page 22. Sew along the

drawn lines, and then trim the seam allowances to ¼". Repeat to make two tree units.

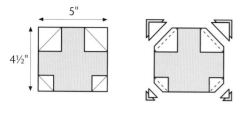

Make 2 units,
4½" × 5".

2. Sew two white solid 2¼" × 3¼" rectangles to the long sides of one brown 1½" × 3¼" rectangle. The trunk unit should measure 3¼" × 5", including the seam allowances.

Make 1 unit,
3¼" × 5".

3. Lay out one white solid 3¼" × 5" rectangle, the two tree units, and the trunk unit. Orient the tree units as shown, matching the small triangles at the center seam. Join the rectangle, tree units, and trunk unit along the long edges. Repeat to make six Tree blocks that measure 5" × 14", including the seam allowances.

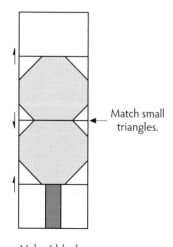

Match small triangles.

Make 6 blocks,
5" × 14".

Making the Pinwheel Blocks

1. Draw a diagonal line from corner to corner on the wrong side of the white solid 2" squares for the Pinwheel blocks. Place one marked square on one end of a red dot 2" × 3½" rectangle, orienting the drawn line as shown. Sew on the drawn line. Trim the seam allowance to ¼"; press. Repeat to sew a second white square to the opposite end of the rectangle. Repeat to make 72 flying-geese units.

Make 72 units,
2" × 3½".

2. Sew a white solid 2" × 3½" rectangle to the top of each flying-geese unit. Make 72. The units should measure 3½" square, including the seam allowances.

Make 72 units,
3½" × 3½".

3. Lay out four pieced units in two rows of two, arranging them in a pinwheel shape. Join the units in each row, and then join the rows to make a Pinwheel block that measures 6½" square, including the seam allowances. Make 18 Pinwheel blocks.

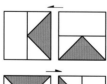

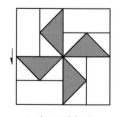

Make 18 blocks,
6½" × 6½".

Assembling the Quilt Top

1. The quilt has three House rows, which each contain three House blocks and two Tree blocks. Determine the desired assortment of House and Tree blocks for each row. Lay out one row of three House blocks alternating with two Tree blocks as shown. Join the blocks. The row should measure 14" × 54½", including the seam allowances. Repeat to make a total of three House rows.

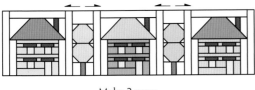

Make 3 rows,
14" × 54½".

2. Lay out nine Pinwheel blocks. Join the blocks. The row should measure 6½" × 54½", including the seam allowances. Make two rows.

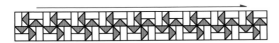

Make 2 rows,
6½" × 54½".

3. Join the aqua dot 2"-wide strips end to end; press the seam allowances in one direction. From the pieced length, cut four strips, 2" × 54½"; two strips, 2" × 57½"; and two strips, 2" × 59".

4. Lay out the three House rows, two Pinwheel rows, and four aqua dot 2" × 54½" strips as shown in the quilt assembly diagram above right. Join the rows and strips. The quilt top should measure 54½" × 59", including the seam allowances.

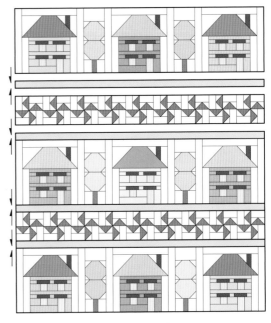

Quilt assembly

5. Sew the aqua dot 2" × 59" strips to the sides of the quilt top, which should now measure 57½" × 59". Press the seam allowances toward the strips. Sew the aqua dot 2" × 57½" strips to the top and bottom of the quilt; press. The quilt top should now measure 57½" × 62", including the seam allowances.

6. Join the white floral strips end to end; press the seam allowances in one direction. From the length, cut two strips, 4½" × 62", and two strips, 4½" × 65½".

7. Sew the short white floral strips to the sides of the quilt; press the seam allowances toward the borders. The quilt top should now measure 62" × 65½". Sew the long border strips to the top and bottom of the quilt; press. The quilt top should measure 65½" × 70".

Finishing the Quilt

Go to ShopMartingale.com/HowtoQuilt for more details on quilting and finishing.

1. Layer the backing, batting, and quilt top; baste the layers together. Hand or machine quilt as desired. The quilt shown was machine quilted with an allover swirl design.

2. Use the red-and-pink stripe 2½"-wide strips to make the binding and then attach it to the quilt.

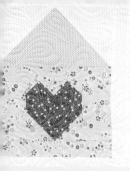

Home Is Where the Heart Is

Adorable houses
dance across the fun
and simple layout
of this quilt. The
easy-to-piece hearts
decorating the houses
and cornerstones are
a perfect reminder of
how quilts can truly fill
a home with love.

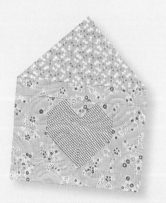

Materials

Yardage is based on 42"-wide fabric. Fat quarters are 18" × 21".

4 yards of white solid for background

13 fat quarters of assorted bright prints for houses: aqua, green, and pink

7 fat quarters of assorted red prints for hearts

¾ yard of red-and-white check for binding

4¾ yards of fabric for pieced backing*

68" × 84" piece of batting

If you follow Melissa's suggestion of piecing the backing from yardage in combination with the extra flying-geese units and House block (see "Piece the Backing" on page 29), 4 yards will be adequate. Otherwise you'll need 4¾ yards.

Cutting

All measurements include ¼" seam allowances.

From the white solid, cut:

❖ 29 strips, 1½" × 42"; crosscut 21 of the strips into:
  25 rectangles, 1½" × 10½"
  25 rectangles, 1½" × 9½"
  36 rectangles, 1½" × 2½"
  72 squares, 1½" × 1½"

❖ 7 strips, 4⅞" × 42"; crosscut into 52 squares, 4⅞" × 4⅞"

❖ 8 strips, 3½" × 42"; crosscut into 30 rectangles, 3½" × 9½"

❖ 10 strips, 2½" × 42"; crosscut into 30 rectangles, 2½" × 11½"

❖ 4 strips, 1" × 42"; crosscut into 144 squares, 1" × 1"

❖ 2 rectangles, 1½" × 16½"*

❖ 2 rectangles, 3½" × 8½"*

These pieces are for an optional pieced backing (see "Piece the Backing").

Continued on page 26

Home Is Where the Heart Is by Melissa Corry
FINISHED QUILT: 59½" × 75½"
FINISHED BLOCK: 9" × 11"

Continued from page 24

From *each* of the assorted bright aqua, green, and pink prints, cut:

- ❖ 1 square, 9¼" × 9¼" (13 total)
- ❖ 4 rectangles, 2½" × 4½" (52 total)
- ❖ 4 squares, 2½" × 2½" (52 total)
- ❖ 4 rectangles, 1½" × 8½" (52 total)
- ❖ 8 squares, 1½" × 1½" (104 total)

From the assorted red prints, cut:

- ❖ 26 matching pairs of 2 rectangles, 2½" × 4½" (52 total)
- ❖ 36 matching pairs of 2 rectangles, 1½" × 2½" (72 total)

From the red-and-white check, *cut on the bias*:

- ❖ 2½"-wide strips, enough to yield 300" of bias binding

Making the Flying-Geese Units

Press all seam allowances in the directions indicated by the arrows.

1. Place two white 4⅞" background squares on diagonally opposite corners of a bright 9¼" square with right sides together, aligning the edges as shown. Carefully draw a line diagonally from the top-left corner to the bottom-right corner of the white squares. Stitch ¼" from both sides of the drawn line. Cut on the drawn line to yield two units. Repeat to make 13 pairs of units.

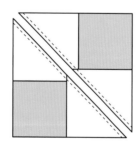

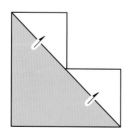

Make 13 pairs.

2. Draw a diagonal line from corner to corner on the wrong side of a white 4⅞" square. Place the marked square on the corner of a unit from step 1 with right sides together, aligning raw edges as shown. Stitch ¼" from both sides of the drawn line. Cut along the line to yield two flying-geese units. Trim the units to measure 4½" × 8½". Repeat to make 52 flying-geese units. You'll need 25 units for the House blocks; the rest are for the pieced quilt backing.

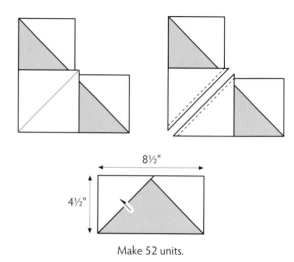

8½"

4½"

Make 52 units.

Making the Heart Units

You'll be making 26 heart units—one for each block, plus one for the quilt back.

1. Draw a diagonal line from corner to corner on the wrong side of the bright print 1½" squares (104 total). Divide the squares into two piles of 52. Each pile should have four squares of each print.

2. Place a marked square on the upper-left corner of a red 2½" × 4½" rectangle as shown with right sides together. Stitch directly on the marked line. Trim ¼" from the seam. Make 52 folded-corner units.

Make 52 units, 2½" × 4½".

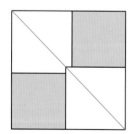

3. Place a matching-print marked square on the adjacent corner of a folded-corner unit as shown. Sew, trim, and press. Make 26 pairs of matching heart units that measure 2½" × 4½", including the seam allowances.

Make 26 matching pairs,
2½" × 4½".

4. Draw a diagonal line from corner to corner on the wrong side of two matching bright 2½" squares. Place one square on the lower section of one heart unit, orienting the line as shown. Sew on the line, and then trim the seam allowance to ¼". Repeat to sew the matching square in the opposite direction on the remaining matching heart unit. Make 26 of each type of unit.

Make 26 units,
2½" × 4½".

Make 26 units,
2½" × 4½".

5. Join matching left and right heart units to form a heart, making sure to match the seam intersections. The unit should measure 4½" square, including the seam allowances. Repeat to make 26 units total (two from each bright print).

Make 26 units,
4½" × 4½".

Assembling the Blocks

1. To make a house unit, select one of the heart units, and then select two bright 2½" × 4½" rectangles and two bright 1½" × 8½" rectangles that all match the selected heart unit. Sew the 2½" × 4½" rectangles to the sides of the heart unit. The unit should measure 4½" × 8½", including the seam allowances. Sew the 1½" × 8½" rectangles to the top and bottom of the unit, which should now measure 6½" × 8½", including the seam allowances. Repeat to make 26 house units.

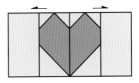

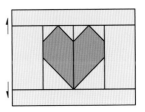

Make 26 units,
6½" × 8½".

2. Pair a house unit with a contrasting flying-geese unit. Sew the flying-geese unit to the top of the house unit. Repeat to make 26 House blocks that measure 8½" × 10½", including the seam allowances.

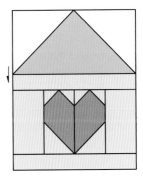

Make 26 blocks,
8½" × 10½".

3. Sew a white 1½" × 10½" rectangle to the left side of a House block. Sew a white 1½" × 9½" rectangle to the bottom of the House block. The block should measure 9½" × 11½", including the seam allowances. Repeat to make 13 House A blocks.

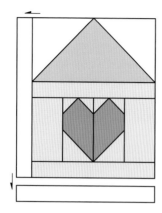

Make 13 A blocks,
9½" × 11½".

4. Sew a white 1½" × 10½" rectangle to the right side of a House block. Sew a white 1½" × 9½" rectangle to the top of the House block. The block should measure 9½" × 11½". Repeat to make 12 House B blocks. Note that you'll have one extra House block, which is for the back of the quilt.

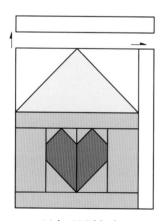

Make 12 B blocks,
9½" × 11½".

Making the Cornerstones

1. Draw a diagonal line on the wrong side of the white 1" squares and 1½" squares. Using the 1" squares and red print 1½" × 2½" rectangles, make 72 cornerstone heart units following the same process as in steps 2 and 3 of "Making the Heart Units" on page 26.

Make 72 units,
1½" × 2½".

2. Using the cornerstone heart units and white 1½" squares, make 36 matching pairs of left and right cornerstone heart units following the same process as in step 4 of "Making the Heart Units."

Make 36 units,
1½" × 2½".

Make 36 units,
1½" × 2½".

3. Join the left and right cornerstone heart-unit pairs as shown, making sure to match the seams. Sew a white 1½" × 2½" rectangle to the top of each unit. The units should measure 2½" × 3½", including the seam allowances. Make 36 cornerstones.

Make 36 cornerstones,
2½" × 3½".

Assembling the Quilt Top

1. Lay out the blocks in five rows of five, alternating the A and B blocks. Place six white 2½" × 11½" rectangles between the blocks in each row as sashing. For the six horizontal sashing rows, alternate six cornerstones and five white 3½" × 9½" rectangles as shown in the quilt assembly diagram below. Alternate the block and horizontal sashing rows as shown.

2. Join the blocks and rectangles in each block row. Join the rectangles and cornerstones in each horizontal sashing row. Join the rows. The quilt top should measure 57½" × 73½", including the seam allowances.

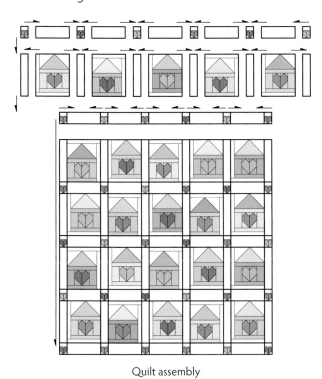

Quilt assembly

3. Join the white 1½" × 42" strips end to end. From the pieced length, cut two strips, 1½" × 57½", and two strips, 1½" × 75½". Sew the short strips to the top and bottom of the quilt top; press the seam allowances toward the strips. The quilt should now measure 57½" × 75½". Sew the long strips to the sides of the quilt top; press. The quilt top should now measure 59½" × 75½".

Finishing the Quilt

Go to ShopMartingale.com/HowtoQuilt for more details on quilting and finishing.

1. Layer the backing, batting, and quilt top; baste the layers together. Hand or machine quilt as desired. The quilt shown was machine quilted with an allover swirling paisley design.

2. Use the red print 2½"-wide strips to make the binding and then attach it to the quilt.

PIECE THE BACKING

Add a special touch to the quilt by using the extra flying geese and House block to make a pieced backing. Sew white 3½" × 8½" rectangles to the top and bottom of the House block. Sew two white 1½" × 16½" rectangles to the sides of the block. Sew the flying-geese units into two panels as shown. Sew the flying-geese panels to the sides of the block. The pieced row should measure 16½" × 62½".

From the backing fabric, cut one rectangle, 42" × 62½", and one rectangle, 18" × 62½", from the lengthwise grain. Sew the large rectangle to the top of the pieced unit, and the small rectangle to the bottom. The pieced backing should measure 62½" × 75½".

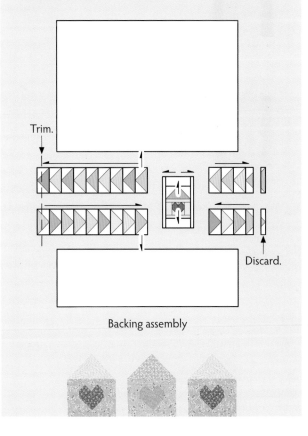

Backing assembly

My Hometown

Even if your hometown doesn't exactly resemble this charming quilt, it's fun to imagine that you live in a quilty neighborhood full of colorful prints. These simple houses are fun and easy to piece from fat quarters.

Materials

Yardage is based on 42"-wide fabric. Fat quarters are 18" × 21" and should have approximately 16" × 18" of usable area.

16 fat quarters of assorted prints for houses*

2⅝ yards of gray solid for background and border

⅝ yard of blue print for binding

3¾ yards of fabric for backing

62" × 66" piece of batting

*For a scrappier variety among the houses, incorporate more prints.

Cutting for the House Blocks

All measurements include ¼" seam allowances. Refer to the cutting diagram below for best use of fat quarters and the "Cut and Label" tip on page 32 to keep pieces organized.

From *each* of the 16 assorted prints, cut:

❖ 2 rectangles, 5" × 7" (F)

❖ 5 strips, 1½" × 16"; crosscut into:
    4 rectangles, 1½" × 2½" (B)
    4 rectangles, 1½" × 4½" (C)
    4 rectangles, 1½" × 4½" (D)
    4 rectangles, 1½" × 6½" (E)

❖ 2 squares, 2½" × 2½" (A)

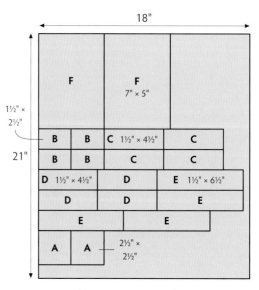

Fat-quarter cutting diagram

My Hometown by Christa Watson
FINISHED QUILT: 55½" × 59½"
FINISHED BLOCK: 6" × 10"

CUT AND LABEL

You should have 32 pieces each of A and F, and 64 pieces each of B, C, D, and E. Label each piece with painter's tape to keep your fabric organized.

Cutting for the Background and Binding

From the gray solid, cut from the *lengthwise* grain:

❖ 1 rectangle, 42" × 60"; crosscut into:
  - 2 strips, 6½" × 60"; crosscut into
    - 32 rectangles, 3½" × 6½"
  - 1 strip, 6" × 60"; crosscut into 8 squares, 6" × 6". Cut the squares in half diagonally to yield 16 G triangles.*
  - 4 strips, 4" × 60"

From the remaining gray solid, cut:

❖ 4 strips, 6" × 42"; crosscut into 24 squares, 6" × 6". Cut the squares in half diagonally to yield 48 G triangles.*

From the blue print, cut:

❖ 6 strips, 2½" × 42"

If the fabric has a right and wrong side, make sure to cut half of the squares diagonally from upper left to lower right and cut the remaining half from upper right to lower left.

Assembling the Log-Cabin Units

Christa recommends pressing the seam allowances open to ensure flatter blocks. If you plan to press the seam allowances open, reduce the stitch length to keep the seams from splitting open. For each House block, choose an A square, matching B

and C rectangles, and matching D and E rectangles that contrast with the B and C rectangles.

1. Sew an A square between two B rectangles. The unit should measure 2½" × 4½", including the seam allowances.

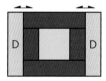

Make 1 unit,
2½" × 4½".

2. Sew the C rectangles to the top and bottom of the unit. The unit should now measure 4½" square, including the seam allowances.

Make 1 unit,
4½" × 4½".

3. Sew the D rectangles to opposite sides of the unit, which should now measure 4½" × 6½", including the seam allowances.

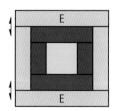

Make 1 unit,
4½" × 6½".

4. Sew the E rectangles to the top and bottom of the unit. The unit should now measure 6½" square, including the seam allowances. Repeat steps 1–4 to make 32 log-cabin units.

Make 32 units,
6½" × 6½".

Paper Piecing the Rooftops

For more details on how to paper piece, go to ShopMartingale.com/HowtoQuilt for free downloadable information. First sew a test block to ensure proper placement of the fabric.

1. Make 32 photocopies of the triangle rooftop foundation pattern on page 34. Cut the paper block patterns approximately ¼" from the outer dashed line.

2. Pin or lightly glue an F rectangle to the nonprinted side of the foundation pattern. Crease the paper along the diagonal line between spaces 1 and 2. Trim the fabric rectangle approximately ¼" beyond lines 1 and 2.

3. Place a G triangle right sides together with its long diagonal lined up with the edge of the trimmed F fabric. Flip the unit over and sew on the line between spaces 1 and 2.

4. Repeat step 3 for the opposite side of the rooftop, placing a second G triangle right sides together and joining the seam on the line between spaces 1 and 3. Repeat to make a total of 32 rooftops that measure 4½" × 6½", including the seam allowances.

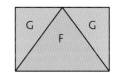

Make 32 rooftop units,
4½" × 6½".

Assembling the House Blocks

1. Sew a rooftop unit to the top of a log-cabin unit. Make 32 House blocks that measure 6½" × 10½", including the seam allowances.

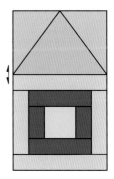

Make 32 blocks,
6½" × 10½".

2. Sew a gray rectangle to the top of 16 blocks and to the bottom of the remaining 16 blocks. The blocks should now measure 6½" × 13½", including the seam allowances.

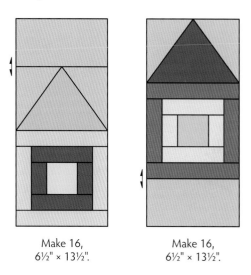

Make 16,
6½" × 13½".

Make 16,
6½" × 13½".

Assembling the Quilt Top

1. Lay out the blocks in four rows of eight, alternating the blocks with top and bottom gray rectangles as shown in the quilt assembly diagram. Join the blocks in each row, and then join the rows. The quilt top should measure 48½" × 52½", including the seam allowances.

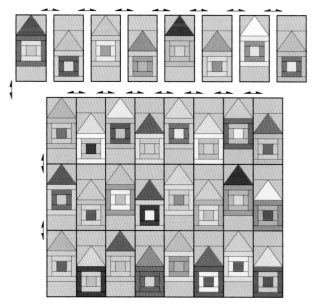

Quilt assembly

2. Trim two of the gray border strips to 4" × 52½", and then sew them to the sides of the quilt top; press the seam allowances toward the strips. The quilt should now measure 52½" × 55½". Trim the remaining border strips to measure 4" × 55½" and sew them to the top and bottom of the quilt top; press. The quilt top should measure 55½" × 59½".

Finishing the Quilt

Go to ShopMartingale.com/HowtoQuilt for more details on quilting and finishing.

1. Layer the backing, batting, and quilt top; baste the layers together. Hand or machine quilt as desired. The quilt shown was machine quilted with a swirl and pebble design in the background and simple wavy lines within the House blocks. See "Machine Quilting Tips," at right, for more information.

2. Use the blue 2½"-wide strips to make the binding and then attach it to the quilt.

MACHINE QUILTING TIPS

If you plan to machine quilt, stitch in the ditch around the houses to secure the quilt layers before doing any free-motion quilting. Then fill in all of the background with free-motion quilting in one pass, working your way around the houses. Quilt each House block completely before moving on to the next. Backtrack as needed to quilt an entire row of House blocks without the need to stop and start between each one.

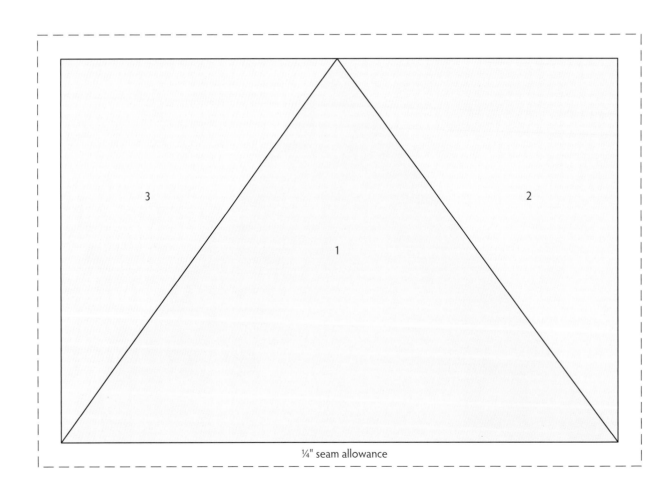

¼" seam allowance

Log Cabin Houses

Materials

Yardage is based on 42"-wide fabric. Fat quarters are 18" × 21".

2 yards of white solid for background

½ yard of black solid for roofs

1 fat quarter of pink solid for pinwheels

5 fat quarters, 1 *each* of assorted solids for houses: yellow, red, blue, navy, and gray

⅝ yard of red solid for binding

3 yards of fabric for backing

52" × 52" square of batting

Cutting

All measurements include ¼" seam allowances.

From the white solid, cut:

❖ 18 strips, 2½" × 42"; crosscut into:
   - 27 rectangles, 1½" × 2½" (A)
   - 36 rectangles, 2½" × 3½" (B)
   - 27 rectangles, 2½" × 4½" (C)
   - 27 rectangles, 2½" × 5½" (D)
   - 91 squares, 2½" × 2½"
   - 27 left triangles*
   - 27 right triangles*

❖ 2 strips, 3" × 42"; crosscut into:
   - 17 squares, 3" × 3"
   - 5 rectangles, 3" × 4"

❖ 6 strips, 1½" × 42"; crosscut into:
   - 6 strips, 1½" × 22"**
   - 18 squares, 1½" × 1½"

From the pink solid, cut:

❖ 2 strips, 3" × 21"; crosscut into 8 squares, 3" × 3"

From the yellow solid, cut:

❖ 3 strips, 2½" × 21"; crosscut into:
   - 18 rectangles, 1½" × 2½" (E)
   - 9 squares, 2½" × 2½"

Use the left and right triangle patterns on page 39.
**See "Simplify the Sewing" on page 38 before cutting.*

Continued on page 37

Do you remember building your dream house from wooden blocks painted in primary colors? This playful Log Cabin–style House block is a tribute to kids and their big imaginations.

Log Cabin Houses by Natalie Barnes
FINISHED QUILT: 45½" × 45½"
FINISHED BLOCK: 15" × 15"

Continued from page 35

From the black solid, cut:

❖ 3 strips, 2½" × 42"; crosscut into:
    9 rectangles, 2½" × 4½"
    9 rectangles, 1½" × 2½"
    27 rooftops***

❖ 2 strips, 3" × 42"; crosscut into:
    5 rectangles, 3" × 4"
    9 squares, 3" × 3"

From the red solid, cut:

❖ 5 strips, 2½" × 21"; crosscut into:
    36 rectangles, 1½" × 2½" (F)
    9 squares, 2½" × 2½"

From the blue solid, cut:

❖ 3 strips, 2½" × 21"; crosscut into 18 squares, 2½" × 2½"

From the navy solid, cut:

❖ 4 strips, 2½" × 21"; crosscut into 27 squares, 2½" × 2½"

From the gray solid, cut:

❖ 5 strips, 2½" × 21"; crosscut into:
    18 rectangles, 1½" × 2½" (G)
    18 squares, 2½" × 2½"

From the red solid for binding, cut:

❖ 6 strips, 2½" × 42"

***Use the rooftop pattern on page 39.*

Making the Block Units

Press all seam allowances in the directions indicated by the arrows.

1. Draw a diagonal line from corner to corner on the wrong side of nine white 3" squares. Place a marked square right sides together with a black 3" square. Sew ¼" from both sides of the drawn line. Cut along the line to yield two half-square-triangle units. Trim each unit to measure 2½" square. Repeat to make 18 half-square-triangle units.

Make 18 units.

2. Repeat the process in step 1 using eight white and eight pink 3" squares to make 16 half-square-triangle units, 2½" square, for the pinwheels.

3. Draw a diagonal line from corner to corner on the wrong side of the white 1½" squares. Place a marked square on one end of a black 1½" × 2½" rectangle, orienting the line as shown. Sew on the line, and then trim the seam allowances to ¼". Press.

Make 9 units, 1½" × 2½".

4. Place a second marked square on the opposite end of the rectangle, orienting the line as shown. Sew, trim, and press. Make nine flying-geese units that measure 1½" × 2½", including the seam allowances.

Make 9 units, 1½" × 2½".

5. Using the process from steps 3 and 4, make a large flying-geese unit using one black 2½" × 4½" rectangle and two white 2½" squares. Repeat to make nine large flying-geese units that measure 2½" × 4½", including the seam allowances.

6. Place a white right triangle on a black rooftop triangle with right sides together as shown. Sew the aligned right edge; press. Repeat to sew a white left triangle to the left edge of the rooftop triangle. The unit should measure 2½" square, including the seam allowances. Repeat to make 27 roof units.

Make 27 units, 2½" × 2½".

7. Draw a diagonal line from the upper-right corner to the bottom-left corner on the wrong side of the white 3" × 4" rectangles. Place a marked rectangle right sides together with a black 3" × 4" rectangle, aligning the marked line with two diagonally opposite corners of the black rectangle as shown; pin. Sew ¼" from both sides of the drawn line. Cut along the marked line to yield two half-rectangle triangles. Trim the units to measure 2½" × 3½". Make nine (one is extra).

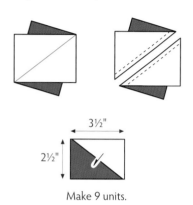

Make 9 units.

8. For the block centers, join three white 1½" × 22" strips along the long edges. Make two strip sets. From each strip set, crosscut 14 segments, 1½" × 3½" (one is extra).

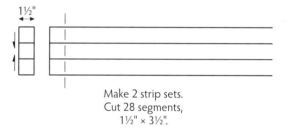

Make 2 strip sets.
Cut 28 segments,
1½" × 3½".

9. Join three strip-set segments along the long edges, nesting the seam allowances at the intersections. Repeat to make nine center units that measure 3½" square, including the seam allowances.

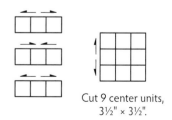

Cut 9 center units,
3½" × 3½".

SIMPLIFY THE SEWING

If you'd prefer to save cutting and sewing time, rather than piecing an all-white Nine Patch for the center of each block, you can simply cut nine 3½" squares to use for block centers.

Assembling the Blocks

All of the blocks in this quilt are laid out and pieced in the same way, *except for the location of the pink triangle that will form part of the pinwheel.* Instructions for the top-left block are given below. Note that the numbers in the block assembly diagram refer to the order in which each unit will be joined to the block center. All of the squares in all of the units are 2½" × 2½". Refer to the block assembly diagram following step 1 for the placement of the various rectangles.

1. Referring to the block assembly diagram below, use a large flat surface or design wall to lay out the pieced units and solid pieces for the upper-left corner block as shown. Carefully remove the pieces in each numbered section from the block layout and join the pieces in each section. Return the sections to the layout after piecing them.

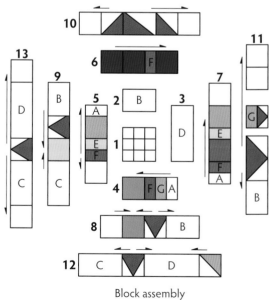

Block assembly
(Upper-left corner block).

2. Join the pieced sections in numerical order, working your way outward from the center. Press the seam allowances toward the section just added. The block should measure 15½" square, including the seam allowances.

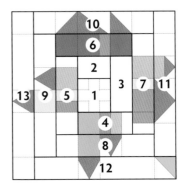

Make 1
(upper-left corner block),
15½" × 15½".

3. Repeat to make a total of nine blocks. Refer to the quilt assembly diagram above right for the placement of the pinwheel half-square triangles and for the orientation of each block, as each one is rotated differently. Use a white 2½" square in place of a pinwheel half-square triangle where applicable.

Assembling the Quilt Top

Arrange the blocks in three horizontal rows of three blocks each, referring to the quilt assembly diagram. Join the blocks, and then join the rows. The quilt top should measure 45½" square.

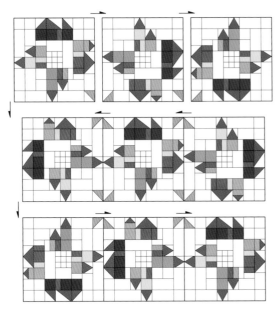

Quilt assembly

Finishing the Quilt

Go to ShopMartingale.com/HowtoQuilt for more details on quilting and finishing.

1. Layer the backing, batting, and quilt top; baste the layers together. Hand or machine quilt as desired. The quilt shown was machine echo quilted within the house shapes and in the center units of the blocks. The background between the houses was quilted with an overall swirl design.

2. Use the red 2½"-wide strips to make the binding and then attach it to the quilt.

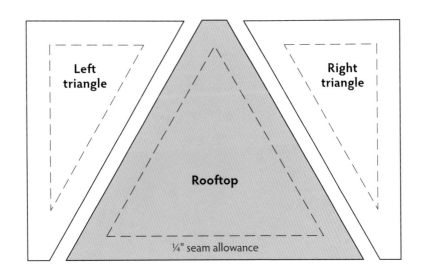

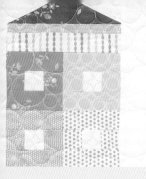

Welcome Home

Choose a sophisticated color palette to make the stately homes in these blocks. Using a stripe fabric for the top section of the house gives the impression of an extra architectural detail.

Materials

Yardage is based on 42"-wide fabric.

½ yard of charcoal print for rooftops

2⅛ yards of white solid for background

⅓ yard *each* of multicolored stripe and assorted prints for houses: white, light coral, bright coral, yellow, gray, and green

⅝ yard of gray dot for binding

3 yards of fabric for backing

49" × 55" piece of batting

Cutting

All measurements include ¼" seam allowances.

From the charcoal print, cut:

❖ 5 strips, 2½" × 42"; crosscut into 20 rectangles, 2½" × 7½"

From the white solid, cut from the *lengthwise* grain:

❖ 8 strips, 2½" × 44½"

From the remaining white solid, cut:

❖ 10 strips, 2½" × 42"; crosscut into:
    20 rectangles, 2½" × 6½"
    40 rectangles, 2½" × 4"

From the white print, cut:

❖ 6 strips, 1½" × 42"; crosscut into 80 squares, 1½" × 1½"

From *each* of the bright coral, yellow, gray, and green prints, cut:

❖ 6 strips, 1½" × 42"; crosscut into:
    40 rectangles, 1½" × 3½"
    40 squares, 1½" × 1½"

From the multicolored stripe, cut:

❖ 5 strips, 1½" × 42"; crosscut into 20 rectangles, 1½" × 6½"

From the light coral print, cut:

❖ 5 strips, 1" × 42"; crosscut into 20 rectangles, 1" × 6½"

From the gray dot, cut:

❖ 6 strips, 2½" × 42"

Welcome Home by Kimberly Jolly and Sarah Price
FINISHED QUILT: 42½" × 48½"
FINISHED BLOCK: 6" × 9"

Making the Rooftops

Press all seam allowances in the directions indicated by the arrows.

1. Use the patterns on page 43 to cut 20 rooftops from the charcoal rectangles and 20 left and 20 right triangles from the white 2½" × 4" rectangles.

2. Sew a left triangle to the left edge of a rooftop triangle; press. Sew a right triangle to the right edge of the rooftop triangle. The rooftop should measure 2" × 6½", including the seam allowances. Make 20 rooftops.

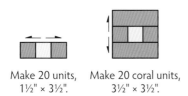

Make 20 rooftops,
2" × 6½".

Making the Blocks

1. Sew a white print square between two bright coral squares. The unit should measure 1½" × 3½", including the seam allowances. Sew the unit between two bright coral 1½" × 3½" strips. The unit should measure 3½" square, including the seam allowances. Repeat to make 20 coral house units.

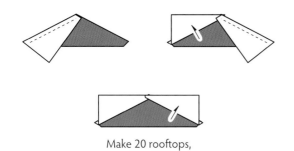

Make 20 units,   Make 20 coral units,
1½" × 3½".   3½" × 3½".

2. Repeat step 1 to make 20 house units *each* from the yellow, gray, and green prints.

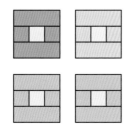

Make 20 units of each color
(80 total).

3. Lay out one unit of each color in two rows of two units. Join the units in each row, and then join the rows. The unit should measure 6½" square, including the seam allowances.

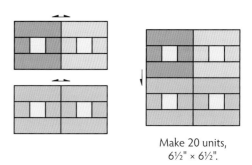

Make 20 units,
6½" × 6½".

4. Lay out a multicolored stripe rectangle, a light coral rectangle, and a rooftop as shown. Join the units. The House block should measure 6½" × 9½", including the seam allowances. Make 20 House blocks.

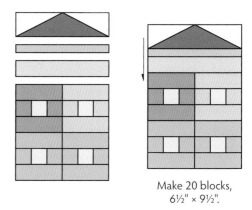

Make 20 blocks,
6½" × 9½".

Assembling the Quilt Top

1. Lay out the blocks in five columns of four blocks each, alternating with white 2½" × 6½" rectangles to create the staggered effect as shown in the quilt assembly diagram on page 43. Note that in columns 1, 3, and 5, the white rectangles are placed below the House blocks. In columns 2 and 4, they're above the blocks.

2. Join the blocks and rectangles in each column. The columns should measure 6½" × 44½".

3. Join the columns and six white 2½" × 44½" strips, alternating them as shown. The quilt top should measure 42½" × 44½", including the seam allowances.

4. Trim the two remaining white strips to 42½" long and sew them to the top and bottom of the quilt; press. The quilt top should measure 42½" × 48½".

Finishing the Quilt

Go to ShopMartingale.com/HowtoQuilt for more details on quilting and finishing.

1. Layer the backing, batting, and quilt top; baste the layers together. Hand or machine quilt as desired. The quilt shown was machine quilted with an allover design of circles in various sizes.

2. Use the gray dot 2½"-wide strips to make the binding and then attach it to the quilt.

Quilt assembly

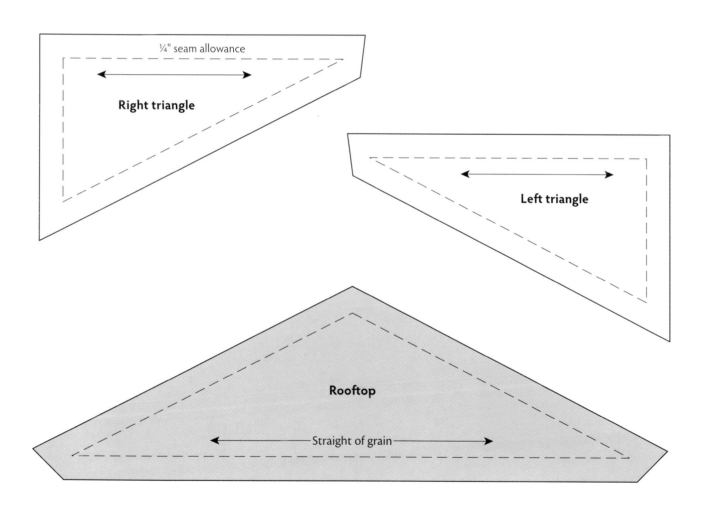

¼" seam allowance

Right triangle

Left triangle

Rooftop

Straight of grain

Tiny Town

Delve into your stash to stitch this scrappy little town. Carrie finds that the cute charm square–friendly House blocks are much like the mini-quilt itself—it's hard to stop with making just one!

Materials
Yardage is based on 42"-wide fabric. Charm squares are 5" × 5".

27 charm squares of assorted dark prints for roofs and houses (9 for roofs, 18 for houses)

¼ yard *total* of assorted light print scraps for background

12 charm squares of assorted light and dark prints for checkerboard rows

½ yard of black print for sashing and border

⅓ yard of red print for binding

⅞ yard of fabric for backing

26" × 30" piece of batting

Cutting
All measurements include scant ¼" seam allowances.

From the 9 assorted dark prints for roofs, cut:
❖ 9 squares, 3½" × 3½"; cut in half diagonally to yield 2 triangles (18 total)

From the light print scraps, cut a *total* of:
❖ 18 squares, 3" × 3"; cut in half diagonally to yield 36 triangles

From *each* of the 18 assorted dark prints for houses, cut:
❖ 3 rectangles, 1½" × 5"; crosscut into:
    2 rectangles, 1½" × 3¼"
    1 rectangle, 1½" × 2¼"
    1 square, 1½" × 1½"

From *each* of the 12 assorted light and dark prints, cut:
❖ 3 strips, 1½" × 5"

From the black print, cut:
❖ 3 strips, 1 × 42"; crosscut into 6 strips, 1" × 18½"
❖ 4 strips, 2¼" × 42"; crosscut into:
    2 strips, 2¼" × 22"
    2 strips, 2¼" × 22¼"

From the red print, cut:
❖ 3 strips, 2½" × 42"

Tiny Town by Carrie Nelson
FINISHED QUILT: 22" × 25¾"
FINISHED BLOCK: 3" × 4¼"

Making the Blocks

Press all seam allowances in the directions indicated by the arrows.

1. Select one roof triangle and a pair of matching light triangles. Sew one light triangle to the left edge of the roof triangle with right sides together, making sure to align the lower triangle points and leave a dog-ear extending at the upper point.

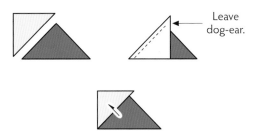

Leave dog-ear.

2. Sew the remaining light triangle to the right edge of the roof triangle with right sides together. Trim away the dog-ear from the first triangle. Trim the unit to 2" × 3½", making sure to leave a ¼" seam allowance at the upper point of the roof. Make 18 roofs.

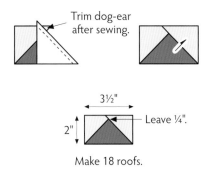

Trim dog-ear after sewing.

3½"

2"

Leave ¼".

Make 18 roofs.

3. Select a matching set of two dark 1½" × 3¼" rectangles and one dark 1½" square for the house. Select a contrasting dark 1½" × 2¼" rectangle for the door. Sew the dark square to one end of the dark 1½" × 2¼" rectangle. The unit should measure 1½" × 3¼", including the seam allowances. Sew the dark rectangles to the sides of the pieced unit. The house unit should measure 3¼" × 3½", including the seam allowances. Repeat to make a total of 18 units.

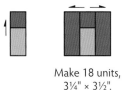

Make 18 units, 3¼" × 3½".

4. Sew one of the roof units to the top of the door. The block should measure 3½" × 4¾", including the seam allowances. Repeat to make a total of 18 House blocks.

Make 18 blocks, 3½" × 4¾".

Assembling the Sashing Strips

1. Join two contrasting 1½" × 5" strips along the long edges. The strip set should measure 2½" × 5". Make 18 strip sets. From each strip set, cut three segments, 1½" wide, for a total of 54 segments.

1½"

Make 18 strip sets.
Cut 3 segments, 1½" wide, from each.

2. Join nine strip segments end to end to make a pieced sashing strip. The strip should measure 1½" × 18½", including the seam allowances. Repeat to make two pieced sashing strips.

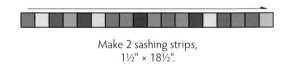

Make 2 sashing strips, 1½" × 18½".

3. Join 18 strip segments along the long edges to make a double-sashing strip that measures 2½" × 18½", including the seam allowances. Repeat to make two double sashing strips.

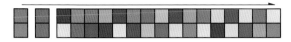

Make 2 double sashing strips,
2½" × 18½".

Assembling the Quilt Top

1. Lay out the House blocks in three rows of six blocks, along with the pieced sashing strips, double sashing strips, and black 1" × 18½" strips as shown in the quilt assembly diagram. Join the blocks in each row, and then join the block rows and all sashing strips. The quilt top should measure 18½" × 22¼", including the seam allowances.

2. Sew the black 2¼" × 22¼" strips to the sides of the quilt top, which should now measure 22" × 22¼", including the seam allowances. Sew the black 2¼" × 22" strips to the top and bottom of the quilt top; press. The quilt top should measure 22" × 25¾".

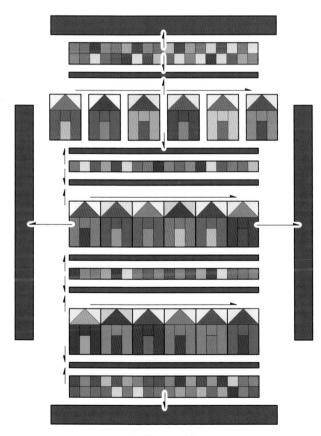

Quilt assembly

Finishing the Quilt

Go to ShopMartingale.com/HowtoQuilt for more details on quilting and finishing.

1. Layer the backing, batting, and quilt top; baste the layers together. Hand or machine quilt as desired. The quilt shown was machine quilted with swirls or feathers within the houses, backgrounds, and roofs, and an X shape in the checkerboard squares.

2. Use the red 2½"-wide strips to make the binding and then attach it to the quilt.

ALTERNATE COLORWAY

Give the quilt a totally different look by using a limited color palette. Carrie chose a scrappy mix of black, white, and orange prints to make this happy Halloween town.

Four Generations

Amanda designed this quilt as a celebration of the four generations of women in her family who all share a love of sewing, represented by the cute clusters of four houses in each block. She took inspiration for the Irish Chain blocks from a treasured quilt she inherited from her great-grandmother.

Materials

Yardage is based on 42"-wide fabric.

2¼ yards of white solid for background

¼ yard *each* of 15 bright prints for blocks*

⅝ yard of blue print for binding

3⅜ yards of fabric for backing

56" × 66" piece of batting

*For a scrappier and more random effect, incorporate more prints.

Cutting

All measurements include ¼" seam allowances.

From the white solid, cut:

❖ 2 strips, 6½" × 42"

❖ 18 strips, 2½" × 42"; crosscut *14* of the strips into:
    30 rectangles, 2½" × 6½"
    120 squares, 2½" × 2½"

❖ 10 strips, 1½" × 42"; crosscut into 30 strips, 1½" × 10½"

From *9* of the bright prints, cut:

❖ 1 strip, 2½" × 42" (9 total)

From *each* of the 15 bright prints, cut:

❖ 4 rectangles, 2½" × 4½" (60 total)

❖ 8 rectangles, 2" × 3½" (120 total)

❖ 4 rectangles, 1½" × 2½" (60 total)

❖ 4 squares, 1½" × 1½" (60 total)

From the blue print, cut:

❖ 6 strips, 2½" × 42"

Four Generations by Amanda Niederhauser
FINISHED QUILT: 50½" × 60½"
FINISHED BLOCKS: 10" × 10"

Making the Irish Chain Blocks

Press all seam allowances in the directions indicated by the arrows.

1. Sew a white 2½" × 42" strip between two different bright 2½" × 42" strips. The strip set should measure 6½" × 42". Make two. From the strip sets, crosscut a total of 30 A segments, 2½" wide.

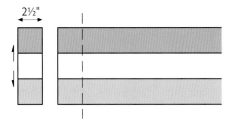

Make 2 strip sets.
Cut 30 A segments, 2½" × 6½".

2. Sew a bright 2½" × 42" strip between two white 2½" × 42" strips. The strip set should measure 6½" × 42". From the strip set, crosscut 15 B segments, 2½" wide.

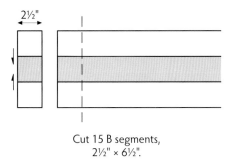

Cut 15 B segments,
2½" × 6½".

3. Sew a B segment between two A segments to make a nine-patch unit. Repeat to make 15 nine-patch units that measure 6½" square, including the seam allowances.

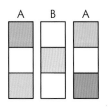

Make 15 units,
6½" × 6½".

4. Sew white 2½" × 6½" rectangles to the top and bottom of a nine-patch unit. The unit should measure 6½" × 10½", including the seam allowances. Make 15.

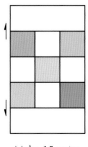

Make 15 units,
6½" × 10½".

5. Sew a white 6½" × 42" strip between two different bright 2½" × 42" strips. The strip set should measure 10½" × 42". Make two. From the strip sets, crosscut a total of 30 segments, 2½" wide.

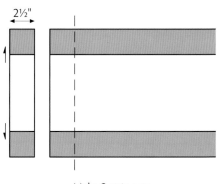

Make 2 strip sets.
Cut 30 segments, 2½" × 10½".

6. Sew one segment from each step 5 strip set to each long side of a unit from step 4. Repeat to make 15 blocks that measure 10½" square, including the seam allowances.

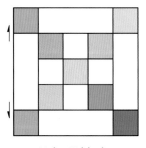

Make 15 blocks,
10½" × 10½".

Making the House Blocks

1. Draw a diagonal line from corner to corner on the wrong side of the white 2½" squares. Place a marked square on one end of a bright 2½" × 4½" rectangle, orienting the drawn line as shown. Sew along the drawn line. Trim the seam allowances to ¼", and then press.

Make 60 units,
2½" × 4½".

2. Place a second square on the opposite end of the rectangle, orienting the line as shown. Sew, trim, and press. The unit should measure 2½" × 4½", including the seam allowances. Make 60 flying-geese units.

Make 60 units,
2½" × 4½".

3. Select a matching set of two bright 2" × 3½" rectangles and one 1½" square. Select a contrasting bright 1½" × 2½" rectangle. Sew the 1½" square to the top of the 1½" × 2½" rectangle. The unit should measure 1½" × 3½", including the seam allowances. Sew the print 2" × 3½" rectangles to the sides of the pieced unit. The house unit should measure 3½" × 4½", including the seam allowances. Make 60 units.

Make 60 units,
3½" × 4½".

4. Sew a contrasting flying-geese unit to the top of each house unit. The house unit should now measure 4½" × 5½", including the seam allowances. Make 60. For easier seam matching in step 5, press the seam allowances on half of the units toward the roofs, and on the other half toward the houses.

Make 60 units,
4½" × 5½".

5. Lay out two rows of two house units. Join the units in each row, and then join the rows. The four-house unit should measure 8½" × 10½", including the seam allowances.

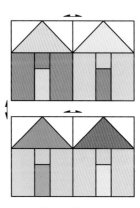

Make 15 units,
8½" × 10½".

6. Sew white 1½" × 10½" strips to the left and right sides of the four-house unit. The block should measure 10½" square, including the seam allowances. Make 15 House blocks.

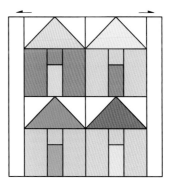

Make 15 blocks,
10½" × 10½".

Assembling the Quilt Top

Lay out the blocks in six rows of five, alternating the Irish Chain and House blocks as shown in the quilt assembly diagram. Join the blocks in each row, and then join the rows, pressing after each step. The quilt top should measure 50½" × 60½".

Finishing the Quilt

Go to ShopMartingale.com/HowtoQuilt for more details on quilting and finishing.

1. Layer the backing, batting, and quilt top; baste the layers together. Hand or machine quilt as desired. The quilt shown was machine quilted with an allover swirl and paisley design.

2. Use the blue 2½"-wide strips to make the binding and then attach it to the quilt.

Quilt assembly

Village on a Hill

Materials

Yardage is based on 42"-wide fabric.

¼ yard *each* of 7 assorted bright solids for houses: blue, orange, light pink, green, dark pink, yellow, and purple

3 yards of white solid for background

¼ yard *each* of 2 shades of pink solids for binding

3⅛ yards of fabric for backing

51" × 73" piece of batting

Cutting

All measurements include ¼" seam allowances. This quilt is made using skinny and fat House blocks. For easier organizing and piecing, the cutting is given for each type of house first, and then cutting for background is listed last.

SKINNY HOUSE BLOCKS

From the assorted bright solids, cut:

❖ 12 rectangles, 3½" × 6½"
❖ 12 rectangles, 3½" × 5½"

From the white solid, cut:

❖ 3 strips, 3½" × 42"; crosscut into 24 squares, 3½" × 3½"
❖ 4 strips, 2" × 42"; crosscut into 24 rectangles, 2" × 5½"

FAT HOUSE BLOCKS

From the assorted bright solids, cut:

❖ 10 rectangles, 2½" × 6½"
❖ 10 rectangles, 4½" × 5½"

From the white solid, cut:

❖ 2 strips, 3½" × 42"; crosscut into 20 squares, 3½" × 3½"
❖ 6 strips, 1½" × 42"; crosscut into:
   10 rectangles, 1½" × 6½"
   20 rectangles, 1½" × 5½"

Continued on page 55

A colorful collection of House blocks in an asymmetrical layout brings to mind a welcoming little village. Choose a spectrum of bright solids to enhance the cheerful feel.

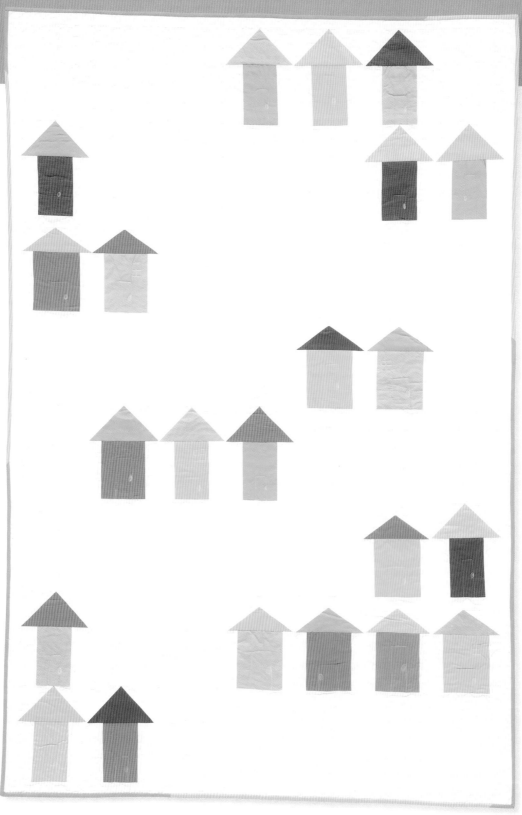

Village on a Hill by Jackie White
FINISHED QUILT: 44½" × 66½"
FINISHED BLOCK: 6" × 8"

Continued from page 53

BACKGROUND AND BINDING

From the white solid, cut:

- ❖ 7 strips, 8½" × 42"; crosscut into:
    - 3 rectangles, 6½" × 8½" (rows 1, 4, and 5)
    - 2 rectangles, 8½" × 24½" (rows 2 and 4)
    - 3 rectangles, 8½" × 30½" (rows 3, 6, and 8)
    - 2 rectangles, 8½" × 18½" (rows 1 and 5)
    - 1 rectangle, 8½" × 12½" (row 7)
- ❖ 6 strips, 1½" × 42"

From *each* of the pink solids for binding, cut:

- ❖ 3 strips, 2½" × 42"

Making the Skinny House Blocks

Press all seam allowances in the directions indicated by the arrows.

1. Sew a bright 3½" × 5½" rectangle between two white 2" × 5½" rectangles along the long edges. The unit should measure 5½" × 6½". Repeat to make 12 skinny house units.

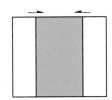

Make 12 units,
5½" × 6½".

2. Draw a diagonal line from corner to corner on the wrong side of 24 white 3½" squares. Place a marked white square on one end of a bright 3½" × 6½" rectangle, orienting the line

as shown. Sew on the drawn line, and then trim the seam allowances to ¼"; press. Make 12 units.

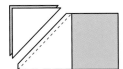

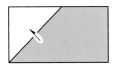

Make 12 units,
3½" × 6½".

3. Place a marked square on the opposite end of the rectangle, and then sew, trim, and press. Make 12 roof units that measure 3½" × 6½", including the seam allowances.

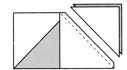

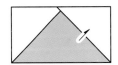

Make 12 units,
3½" × 6½".

4. Pair the house and roof units in the desired color combinations. Sew a roof unit to the top of each house unit. The blocks should measure 6½" × 8½", including the seam allowances. Make 12 Skinny House blocks.

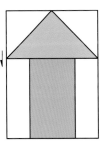

Make 12 blocks,
6½" × 8½".

Making the Fat House Blocks

1. To make the fat house units, sew a bright 4½" × 5½" rectangle between two of the white 1½" × 5½" rectangles to make units that measure 5½" × 6½", including the seam allowances. Make 10.

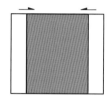

Make 10 units,
5½" × 6½".

2. With right sides together, place a white 3½" square right side down on one end of a bright 2½" × 6½" rectangle, aligning the top and side edges as shown. The bottom edge of the square will extend beyond the rectangle. Draw a line on the square as shown, from the inner-top corner of the square to the lower-right corner of the rectangle. Sew on the line and then trim only the white square ¼" from the line as shown.

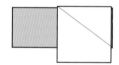

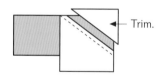

Trim.

3. Press the square away from the rectangle, and then trim the edges of the square evenly with the rectangle. The unit should measure 2½" × 6½". Trim the seam allowances to ¼". Repeat to stitch a second square to the opposite side of the rectangle, and then press and trim it in the same manner. Make 10 units.

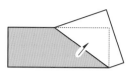

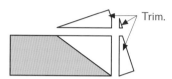

Trim.

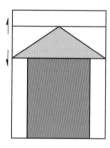

Make 10 units,
2½" × 6½".

4. Sew a roof unit to each fat house unit, pairing the colors as desired. The units should measure 6½" × 7½", including the seam allowances. Sew a white 1½" × 6½" strip to the top of each unit to make 10 Fat House blocks.

Make 10 blocks,
6½" × 8½".

MAKE YOUR VILLAGE UNIQUE

While most of the fat houses have short roofs, you may notice that Jackie gave one of her fat houses a tall roof, as shown in row 5 of the quilt assembly diagram on page 57. Feel free to mix and match the house and roof styles as you like to make your village your own!

Assembling the Quilt Top

1. Lay out the blocks and white background pieces in eight rows as shown in the quilt assembly diagram. Join the blocks and strips in each row, and then join the rows. The quilt top should measure 42½" × 64½", including the seam allowances.

2. Join the white 1½" strips end to end. From the pieced length, cut two strips 64½" long and two strips 44½" long. Sew the long strips to the sides of the quilt top; press the seam allowances toward the strips. Sew the short strips to the top and bottom of the quilt top; press. The quilt top should measure 44½" × 66½".

Finishing the Quilt

Go to ShopMartingale.com/HowtoQuilt for more details on quilting and finishing.

1. Layer the backing, batting, and quilt top; baste the layers together. Hand or machine quilt as desired. The quilt shown was machine quilted with an allover stippling design in the background. The houses were outlined and free-motion quilted with a door motif to add detail.

2. Use the pink 2½"-wide strips to make the scrappy binding and then attach it to the quilt.

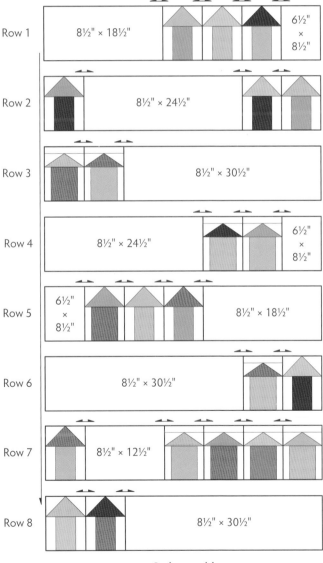

Quilt assembly

Neighborhood

Gather a bright collection of prints to make this friendly neighborhood of scrappy houses. Whip up a charming small quilt to decorate your home or to give as a thoughtful housewarming present.

Materials

Yardage is based on 42"-wide fabric. Fat eighths are 9" × 21".

8 to 12 fat eighths (2 yards total) of assorted prints for sky, houses, doors, and roofs: blue, mint, navy, red, orange, and tan

5" squares or scraps of 3 assorted cream prints for windows

¼ yard *total* of assorted chartreuse prints for grass

½ yard of cream solid for sashing

½ yard of mint print for cornerstones and border

⅜ yard of red print for binding

1⅜ yards of fabric for backing*

42" × 42" square of batting

*If your backing fabric is less than 42" wide, you will need 2 lengths (2¾ yards) to make a backing that is wide enough.

Cutting for 1 House Block

All measurements include ¼" seam allowances. The quilt contains 9 blocks. For each block, select 1 print each for the sky, roof, house, and door. Select 1 chartreuse print for the grass and 1 cream print for the window.

From the sky print, cut:
❖ 2 squares, 3½" × 3½"

From the roof print, cut:
❖ 1 rectangle, 3½" × 9½"

From the window print, cut:
❖ 1 square, 2" × 2"

From the house print, cut:
❖ 1 rectangle, 2" × 9½"
❖ 1 rectangle, 3½" × 4¼"
❖ 1 rectangle, 2" × 4¼"
❖ 2 rectangles, 1⅝" × 2"

From the door print, cut:
❖ 1 rectangle, 2" × 3½"

From the grass print, cut:
❖ 1 rectangle, 2" × 9½"

Neighborhood by Sherri McConnell; machine quilted by Nathel Slater
FINISHED QUILT: 38" × 38"
FINISHED BLOCK: 9" × 9"

Cutting for the Sashing, Borders, and Binding

From the cream solid, cut:

❖ 4 strips, 1½" × 42"; crosscut into:
    2 strips, 1½" × 32"
    2 strips, 1½" × 30"
❖ 3 strips, 1¾" × 42"; crosscut into 12 strips, 1¾" × 9½"

From the mint print, cut:

❖ 4 strips, 3½" × 42"; crosscut into:
    2 strips, 3½" × 38"
    2 strips, 3½" × 32"
❖ 1 strip, 1¾" × 9"; crosscut into 4 squares, 1¾" × 1¾"

From the red print, cut:

❖ 4 strips, 2½" × 42"

Making the House Blocks

Press all seam allowances in the directions indicated by the arrows.

1. Draw a diagonal line from corner to corner on the wrong side of the two sky squares. Place one marked square on one end of the roof rectangle. Sew on the drawn line, and then trim the seam allowances to ¼"; press. Repeat to sew the remaining sky square to the opposite end of the rectangle. The unit should measure 3½" × 9½", including the seam allowances.

Make 1 unit,
3½" × 9½".

2. Sew the window square between two house 1⅝" × 2" rectangles. The unit should measure 2" × 4¼", including the seam allowances. Sew the house 2" × 4¼" rectangle to the bottom of the window unit. The unit should measure 3½" × 4¼", including the seam allowances.

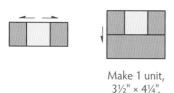

Make 1 unit,
3½" × 4¼".

3. Sew the door rectangle to the right side of the house 3½" × 4¼" rectangle. The door unit should measure 3½" × 5¾", including the seam allowances.

Make 1 unit,
3½" × 5¾".

4. Sew the door unit to the left side of the window unit. The unit should measure 3½" × 9½", including the seam allowances. Sew the house 2" × 9½" rectangle to the top of the house unit. The house unit should measure 5" × 9½", including the seam allowances.

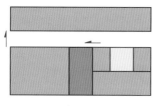

Make 1 unit,
5" × 9½".

5. Sew the roof to the top of the house unit. Sew the grass rectangle to the bottom of the house unit. The block should measure 9½" square, including the seam allowances. Repeat steps 1–5 to make nine blocks.

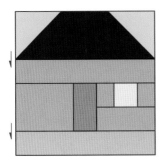

Make 9 blocks,
9½" × 9½".

Assembling the Quilt Top

1. To make the two sashing strips, lay out three cream 1¾" × 9½" strips alternating with two mint 1¾" squares. Join the strips and squares. Repeat to make two sashing strips.

Make 2 sashing strips,
1¾" × 30".

2. Lay out three rows of three blocks alternating with two cream 1¾" × 9½" strips as shown in the quilt assembly diagram above right. Join the blocks and strips. Place the sashing strips from step 1 between the rows. Join the block and sashing rows. The quilt top should measure 30" square, including the seam allowances.

3. Sew the cream 1½" × 30" strips to the sides of the quilt, and then sew the cream 1½" × 32"

PRESSING MATTERS

If you prefer to press seam allowances to one side rather than open, press all of the quilt assembly seam allowances toward the cream sashing strips.

strips to the top and bottom of the quilt. The quilt top should measure 32" square, including the seam allowances.

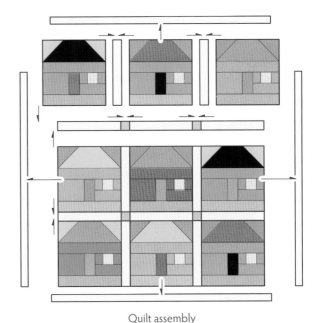

Quilt assembly

4. Sew the mint 3½" × 32" strips to the sides of the quilt top. Press the seam allowances toward the strips. The quilt top should measure 32" × 38", including the seam allowances. Sew the mint 3½" × 38" strips to the top and bottom of the quilt. Press. The quilt top should measure 38" square.

Finishing the Quilt

Go to ShopMartingale.com/HowtoQuilt for more details on quilting and finishing.

1. Layer the backing, batting, and quilt top; baste the layers together. Hand or machine quilt as desired. The quilt shown was machine quilted to highlight the different areas of the quilt, including a scalloped design in the roofs to resemble shingles, a grid pattern in the houses to resemble bricks, swirls in the grass, parallel lines in the border, and a squiggly line design in the sashing.

2. Use the red 2½"-wide strips to make the scrappy binding and then attach it to the quilt.

Suburbia

The layout of this design resembles an orderly map of a peaceful suburb. Use as many different prints and colors as you can find in your stash to add character to the tiny scrappy houses.

Materials

Yardage is based on 42"-wide fabric.

6½ yards of white solid for background

2⅛ yards of blue solid for chain blocks and binding

⅞ yard of black solid for rooftops

⅞ yard *total* of assorted prints for houses

⅛ yard of red solid for cornerstones

5½ yards of fabric for backing

80" × 91" piece of batting

Cutting

All measurements include ¼" seam allowances.

From the white solid, cut:

❖ 48 strips, 2½" × 42"; crosscut:
  33 of the strips into a total of 503 squares, 2½" × 2½"
  7 of the strips into a total of 168 rectangles, 1½" × 2½"
  Reserve 8 of the strips for the border

❖ 59 strips, 1½" × 42"; crosscut 33 of the strips into 97 strips, 1½" × 10½"

From the blue solid, cut:

❖ 11 strips, 2½" × 42"; crosscut 3 of the strips into 42 squares, 2½" × 2½". Reserve the remaining 8 strips for binding.

❖ 26 strips, 1½" × 42"

From the black solid, cut:

❖ 11 strips, 2½" × 42"; crosscut into 168 squares, 2½" × 2½"

From the assorted prints, cut:

❖ 168 squares, 2½" × 2½"

From the red solid, cut:

❖ 56 squares, 1½" × 1½"

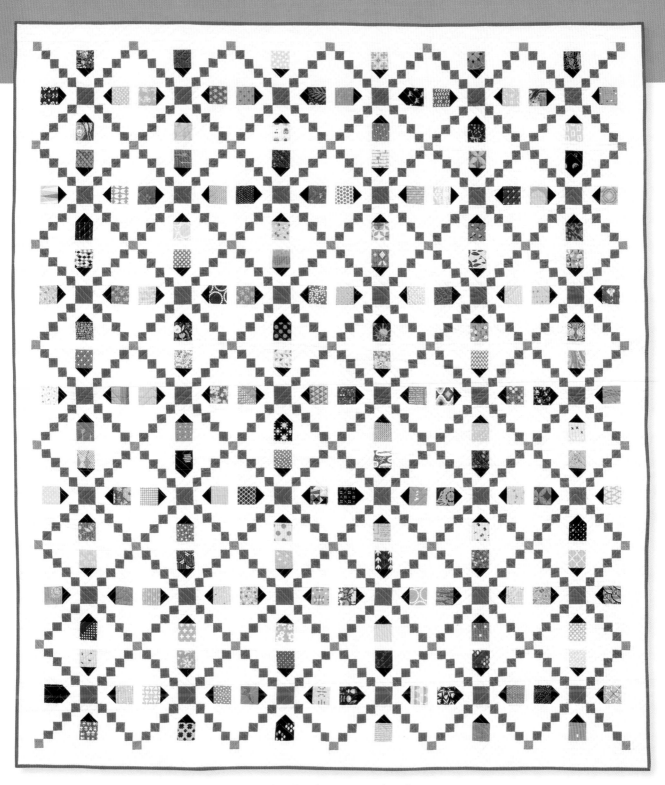

Suburbia by Dana Bolyard
FINISHED QUILT: 71½" × 82½"
FINISHED BLOCK: 10" × 10"

Making the Blocks

Press all seam allowances in the directions indicated by the arrows.

1. Sew one white and one blue 1½" × 42" strip together along the long edges. The strip set should measure 2½" × 42". Repeat to make 26 strip sets. From the strip sets, cut 672 segments, 1½" wide.

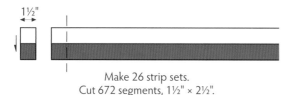

Make 26 strip sets.
Cut 672 segments, 1½" × 2½".

2. Join two segments from step 1 as shown, placing the blue and white squares opposite each other to make a four-patch unit. The unit should measure 2½" square, including the seam allowances. Make 336 four-patch units.

Make 336 units,
2½" × 2½".

3. Lay out two four-patch units and two white 2½" squares in two rows. Join the units in each row, and then join the rows. The unit should measure 4½" square, including the seam allowances. Make 168 double four-patch units.

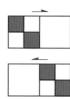

Make 168 units,
4½" × 4½".

4. Draw a line from corner to corner on the wrong side of a white 2½" square. Place the marked square right sides together with a black 2½" square. Sew ¼" from both sides of the drawn line. Cut along the line to yield two half-square-triangle units. The units are slightly oversized for easier sewing; trim them to measure 1½" square. Make 336 half-square-triangle units.

Make 336.

5. Join two half-square-triangle units to make a roof unit as shown. The roof unit should measure 1½" × 2½", including the seam allowances. Make 168 roof units.

Make 168 units,
1½" × 2½".

6. Join one white 1½" × 2½" rectangle, one roof unit, and one 2½" print square as shown. The house unit should measure 2½" × 4½", including the seam allowances. Make 168 house units.

Make 168 house units,
2½" × 4½".

7. Lay out four double four-patch units, four house units, and one blue 2½" square in three rows of three. Orient all of the house units with the rooftops pointing toward the center blue square. Join the units in each row, and then join the rows. The block should measure 10½" square, including the seam allowances. Make 42 blocks.

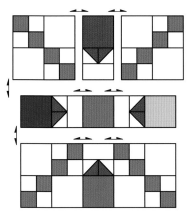

Make 42 blocks,
10½" × 10½".

Assembling the Quilt Top

1. Lay out seven rows of six blocks alternating with seven white 1½" × 10½" strips. Join the blocks and strips. The rows should measure 10½" × 67½", including the seam allowances. Make seven rows.

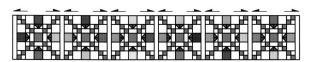

Make 7 rows,
10½" × 67½".

2. For the horizontal sashing rows, lay out six white 1½" × 10½" strips alternating with seven red 1½" squares. Join the strips and squares. The row should measure 1½" × 67½", including the seam allowances. Make eight sashing rows.

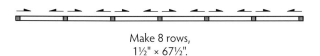

Make 8 rows,
1½" × 67½".

3. Lay out the seven block rows alternating with the eight sashing rows. Join the rows. The quilt top should measure 67½" × 78½", including the seam allowances.

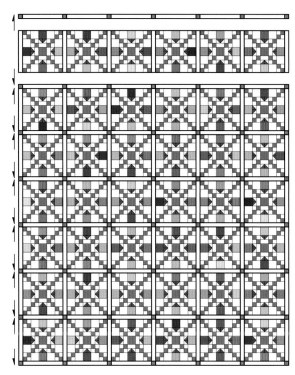

Quilt assembly

4. Join two white 2½" × 42" strips end to end. Repeat to make four long strips. From the strips, cut two 78½" strips and two 71½" strips. Sew the long strips to the sides of the quilt top; press the seam allowances toward the strips. The quilt top should measure 71½" × 78½", including the seam allowances. Sew the short strips to the top and bottom of the quilt top, which should now measure 71½" × 82½".

Finishing the Quilt

Go to ShopMartingale.com/HowtoQuilt for more details on quilting and finishing.

1. Layer the backing, batting, and quilt top; baste the layers together. Hand or machine quilt as desired. The quilt shown was machine quilted with a diamond grid design to emphasize the diagonal lines of the patchwork.

2. Use the remaining blue 2½"-wide strips to make the binding and then attach it to the quilt.

Sugar Shack

Make a bold statement with big and bright houses. The quilt top comes together quickly from just 12 blocks with a simple and graphic house design.

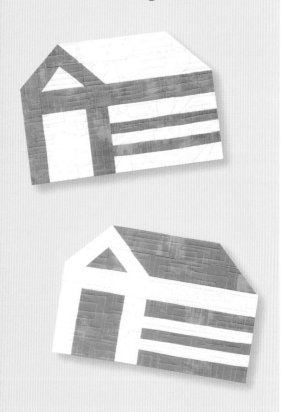

Materials

Yardage is based on 42"-wide fabric.

½ yard *each* of assorted tone on tones for houses and backgrounds: pink, aqua, sky blue, light green, dark green, and dark blue

½ yard *each* of 6 assorted light prints for houses and backgrounds

⅔ yard of blue print for binding

4⅛ yards of fabric for backing

69" × 73" piece of batting

Cutting for 1 House Block

All measurements include ¼" seam allowances. The quilt contains 12 House blocks, 6 with light-print backgrounds and tone-on-tone houses and 6 with tone-on-tone backgrounds and light-print houses. Determine the print pairings before cutting the pieces for each block.

From the house print, cut:
❖ 1 rectangle, 4½" × 6½"
❖ 3 squares, 3½" × 3½"
❖ 2 rectangles, 2½" × 8½"
❖ 2 rectangles, 2" × 10½"
❖ 1 rectangle, 1½" × 10½"

From the background print, cut:
❖ 3 squares, 3½" × 3½"
❖ 1 rectangle, 2½" × 16½"
❖ 2 rectangles, 2½" × 12½"
❖ 2 rectangles, 2½" × 20½"
❖ 1 rectangle, 2½" × 6½"
❖ 2 squares, 2½" × 2½"
❖ 2 rectangles, 1½" × 10½"

From the blue print, cut:
❖ 7 strips, 2½" × 42"

Sugar Shack by Tonya Alexander
FINISHED QUILT: 60½" × 64½"
FINISHED BLOCK: 16" × 20"

Making the House Blocks

Press all seam allowances in the directions indicated by the arrows.

1. Draw a diagonal line from corner to corner on the wrong side of the background 3½" squares. Place a background square right sides together with one house 3½" square. Sew ¼" from both sides of the drawn line. Cut along the line to yield two half-square triangles. Trim the units to measure 2½" square. Repeat to make six half-square-triangle units.

Make 6 units.

2. Join the house 4½" × 6½" rectangle to the left side of the background 2½" × 6½" rectangle. The unit should measure 6½" square, including the seam allowances.

Make 1 unit,
6½" × 6½".

3. Lay out two house 2" × 10½" rectangles and one house 1½" × 10½" rectangle alternating with two background 1½" × 10½" rectangles. Join the rectangles along the long edges. The unit should measure 6½" × 10½", including the seam allowances.

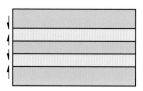

Make 1 unit,
6½" × 10½".

4. Join the unit from step 2 to the left side of the unit from step 3 to make the lower house section, which should measure 6½" × 16½", including the seam allowances.

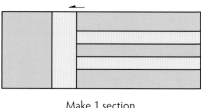

Make 1 section,
6½" × 16½".

5. Lay out the six half-square-triangle units, two background 2½" squares, and two house 2½" × 8½" rectangles as shown in two rows. Make sure to orient the half-square-triangle units to create the diagonal lines of the roof. Join the units in each row. The rows should each measure 2½" × 16½", including the seam allowances.

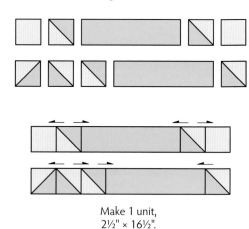

Make 1 unit,
2½" × 16½".

6. Lay out the roof rows, background 2½" × 16½" rectangle, and lower house section in four rows as shown. Join the rows. The house unit should measure 12½" × 16½", including the seam allowances.

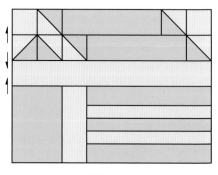

Make 1 unit,
12½" × 16½".

7. Sew the background 2½" × 12½" rectangles to the sides of the block. The block should measure 12½" × 20½". Sew the background 2½" × 20½" rectangles to the top and bottom of the block. The block should measure 16½" × 20½", including the seam allowances. Repeat to make 12 blocks total.

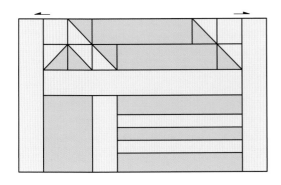

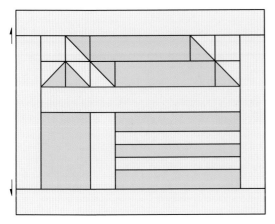

Make 12 blocks,
16½" × 20½".

Assembling the Quilt Top

Lay out the blocks in four rows of three blocks as shown, alternating the light and dark backgrounds. Join the blocks in each row, and then join the rows. The quilt top should measure 60½" × 64½".

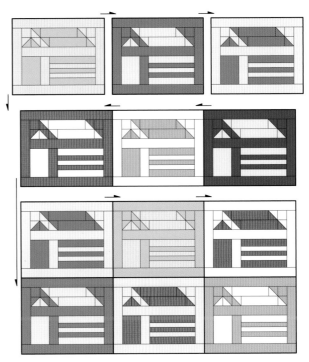

Quilt assembly

Finishing the Quilt

Go to ShopMartingale.com/HowtoQuilt for more details on quilting and finishing.

1. Layer the backing, batting, and quilt top; baste the layers together. Hand or machine quilt as desired. The quilt shown was machine quilted with an allover rectangular stippling design.

2. Use the blue 2½"-wide strips to make the binding and then attach it to the quilt.

The Street Where You Live

"On the Street Where You Live" is a song from the classic musical My Fair Lady. Melissa was inspired by the film's wonderful British row houses with little picket fences, and loved the idea of making them in rich and beautiful colors befitting Eliza Doolittle's stunning dresses.

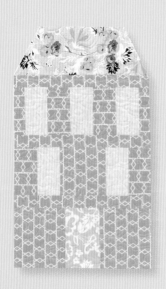

Materials

Yardage is based on 42"-wide fabric. Fat quarters are 18" × 21".

2 yards of white solid for background

12 fat quarters of assorted prints for houses: coral, pink, black, orange, and gray

3 fat quarters of assorted light prints for windows

⅔ yard of black-and-white stripe for binding

4½ yards of fabric for backing

73" × 81" piece of batting

Cutting

All measurements include ¼" seam allowances.

From the white solid, cut:

❖ 7 strips, 3½" × 42"
❖ 3 strips, 6½" × 20½"
❖ 3 strips, 4½" × 20½"
❖ 3 strips, 3½" × 20½"
❖ 3 strips, 2½" × 20½"
❖ 3 strips, 1½" × 20½"
❖ 12 rectangles, 3" × 5"

From *each* of the 12 assorted prints, cut:

❖ 1 rectangle, 4½" × 12½"
❖ 3 rectangles, 1½" × 12½"
❖ 2 rectangles, 5" × 5½"
❖ 1 rectangle, 3½" × 5½"

From the remainder of *3* of the assorted prints, cut for House A:

❖ 1 square, 4½" × 4½"
❖ 4 rectangles, 2½" × 4½"
❖ 2 rectangles, 1½" × 4½"

From the remainder of *3* of the assorted prints, cut for House B:

❖ 1 square, 4½" × 4½"
❖ 2 rectangles, 3½" × 4½"
❖ 3 rectangles, 2½" × 4½"

Continued on page 72

The Street Where You Live by Melissa Corry
FINISHED QUILT: 64½" × 72½"
FINISHED BLOCK: 12" × 20"

Continued from page 70

From the remainder of *3* of the assorted prints, cut for House C:

❖ 2 rectangles, 3½" × 4½"

❖ 3 rectangles, 2½" × 4½"

❖ 2 rectangles, 1½" × 4½"

From the remainder of *3* of the assorted prints, cut for House D:

❖ 1 square, 4½" × 4½"

❖ 4 rectangles, 2½" × 4½"

❖ 2 rectangles, 1½" × 4½"

From the assorted light prints, cut a *total* of:

❖ 57 rectangles, 2½" × 4½"

From the black-and-white stripe, cut:

❖ 8 strips, 2½" × 42"

Making the House Blocks

All of the houses in this quilt are the same size, but there are four different window arrangements, so the houses are labeled A, B, C, and D. Make three of each. Throughout, press the seam allowances as indicated by the arrows.

ROOF AND DOOR UNITS

1. Cut six of the white 3" × 5" rectangles in half from the top-right corner to the bottom-left corner to yield 12 triangles. Cut the remaining six rectangles in half from the top-left corner to the bottom-right corner to yield 12 triangles.

2. Mark 2⅝" in from the top-right and top-left corners on the wrong side of a print 4½" × 12½" rectangle. Align the ruler with the bottom-left corner of the rectangle and the left mark, and then trim the rectangle. Repeat to trim the right side.

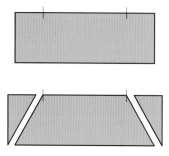

3. Place a white triangle on the left side of the rectangle with right sides together, allowing ¼" to extend above and below the rectangle. Sew the triangle to the rectangle. Repeat to sew an opposite triangle to the right side of the rectangle. Make 12 roof units.

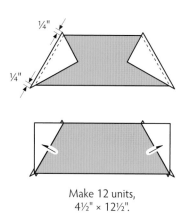

Make 12 units,
4½" × 12½".

4. Select two matching print 5" × 5½" rectangles and one contrasting print 3½" × 5½" rectangle. Join the rectangles as shown. The unit should measure 5½" × 12½", including the seam allowances. Make 12 door units.

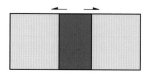

Make 12 units,
5½" × 12½".

WINDOWS FOR HOUSE A

1. Select five matching light 2½" × 4½" rectangles. From one of the house prints, select a matching set of one 4½" square, four 2½" × 4½" rectangles, two 1½" × 4½" rectangles, and one 1½" × 12½" rectangle. Lay out the window and house pieces in three rows as shown.

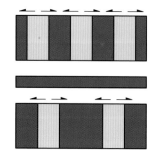

2. Join the pieces in each row, and then join the rows. The unit should measure 9½" × 12½", including the seam allowances. Make three window units for House A.

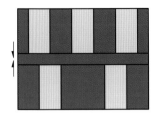

Make 3 A units,
9½" × 12½".

WINDOWS FOR HOUSE B

1. Select four matching light 2½" × 4½" rectangles. From one of the house prints, select a matching set of one 4½" square, two 3½" × 4½" rectangles, three 2½" × 4½" rectangles, and one 1½" × 12½" rectangle. Lay out the window and house pieces in three rows as shown.

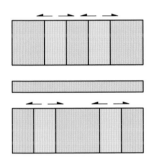

2. Join the pieces in each row, and then join the rows. The unit should measure 9½" × 12½", including the seam allowances. Make three window units for House B.

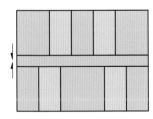

Make 3 B units,
9½" × 12½".

WINDOWS FOR HOUSE C

1. Select five matching light 2½" × 4½" rectangles. From one of the house prints, select a matching set of two 3½" × 4½" rectangles, three 2½" × 4½" rectangles, two 1½" × 4½" rectangles, and one 1½" × 12½" rectangle. Lay out the window and house pieces in three rows as shown.

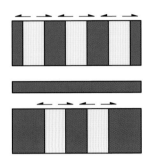

2. Join the pieces in each row, and then join the rows. The unit should measure 9½" × 12½", including the seam allowances. Make three window units for House C.

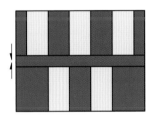

Make 3 C units,
9½" × 12½".

WINDOWS FOR HOUSE D

1. Select five matching light 2½" × 4½" rectangles. From one of the house prints, select a matching set of one 4½" square, four 2½" × 4½" rectangles, two 1½" × 4½" rectangles, and one 1½" × 12½" rectangle. Lay out the window and house pieces in three rows as shown.

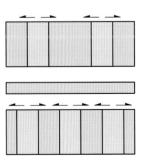

2. Join the pieces in each row, and then join the rows. The unit should measure 9½" × 12½", including the seam allowances. Make three window units for House D.

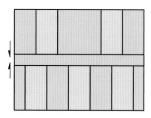

Make 3 D units,
9½" × 12½".

HOUSE BLOCK ASSEMBLY

Lay out one roof unit, one door unit, one window unit, and two print rectangles, 1½" × 12½", that match the house fabric in the window unit as shown. Join the rows. The block should measure 12½" × 20½", including the seam allowances. Make 12 blocks.

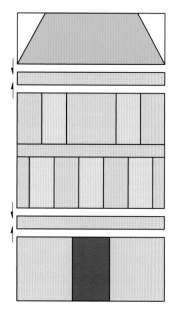

Make 12 blocks,
12½" × 20½".

Assembling the Quilt Top

1. Lay out a row of four House blocks alternating with 20½"-long sashing strips, using one of *each size* of sashing strip. Lay out three rows of four blocks and five sashing strips each. Rearrange the placement of the blocks and sashing strips until you're pleased with the layout. Join the blocks and strips in each row. The rows should measure 20½" × 64½".

2. Sew seven white 3½" × 42" strips together end to end. From the length, cut four strips, 3½" × 64½". Place the strips between the block rows as well as at the top and bottom of the quilt layout. Join the blocks and strips. The quilt top should measure 64½" × 72½".

Quilt assembly

Finishing the Quilt

Go to ShopMartingale.com/HowtoQuilt for more details on quilting and finishing.

1. Layer the backing, batting, and quilt top; baste the layers together. Hand or machine quilt as desired. The quilt shown was machine quilted with an allover curl and swirl design.

2. Use the stripe 2½"-wide strips to make the binding and then attach it to the quilt.

Little Country Home

Materials

Yardage is based on 42"-wide fabric. Fat eighths measure 9" × 21".

8 fat eighths of assorted light prints for sky*

10 fat eighths of assorted dark prints for houses: 3 gold, 2 red, 2 brown, 1 green, 1 blue, and 1 orange*

⅜ yard of black print for doors, roofs, and border

½ yard of antiqued Osnaburg fabric for embroidery blocks

⅓ yard of brown stripe for binding

¾ yard of fabric for backing

26" × 37" piece of batting

7 pieces, 7" × 7", of low-loft batting or fusible interfacing, for backs of embroidery blocks

Wool or cotton embroidery thread: dark and medium brown, soft pink, medium gold, and green

Hand-embroidery needle

Water-soluble pen

You may instead substitute scraps no smaller than 6" × 10".

Cutting

All measurements include ¼" seam allowances.

From *each* of the 8 light prints, cut:

❖ 4 squares, 2½" × 2½" (32 total)

From *1* of the red prints, cut:

❖ 2 rectangles, 2½" × 4½"
❖ 4 rectangles, 2" × 2½"

From the remaining red print, cut:

❖ 1 rectangle, 2½" × 4½"
❖ 2 rectangles, 2" × 2½"

From *1* of the gold prints, cut:

❖ 2 rectangles, 2½" × 4½"
❖ 4 rectangles, 2" × 2½"

Continued on page 77

This little House block brings to mind an old country cottage. Picture a sweet garden with sunflowers, a favorite tree, and birds singing nearby. The hand embroidery adds a warm, personal touch.

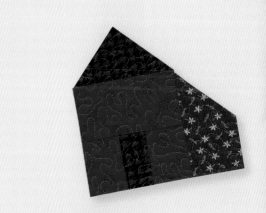

Little Country Home by Jeni Gaston
FINISHED QUILT: 21½" × 33½"
FINISHED BLOCK: 6" × 6"

Continued from page 75

From *each* of the remaining 2 gold prints, cut:

❖ 2 rectangles, 2½" × 4½" (4 total)

From the blue print, cut:

❖ 2 rectangles, 2½" × 4½"
❖ 4 rectangles, 2" × 2½"

From the green print, cut:

❖ 1 rectangle, 2½" × 4½"
❖ 2 rectangles, 2" × 2½"

From *1* of the brown prints, cut:

❖ 2 rectangles, 2½" × 4½"

From the remaining brown print, cut:

❖ 1 rectangle, 2½" × 4½"

From the orange print, cut:

❖ 1 rectangle, 2½" × 4½"

From the black print, cut:

❖ 1 strip, 2½" × 42"; crosscut into:
    8 rectangles, 2½" × 4½"
    8 rectangles, 1½" × 2½"
❖ 4 strips, 2" × 42"; crosscut into:
    2 strips, 2" × 30½"
    2 strips, 2" × 21½"

From the antiqued Osnaburg fabric, cut:

❖ 2 strips, 7" wide; crosscut into 7 squares, 7" × 7"

From the brown stripe, cut:

❖ 3 strips, 2½" × 42"

TO DYE FOR

Jeni suggests staining the Osnaburg fabric to create a warmer, richer shade of light brown. Mix about two cups of hot water in a spray bottle with a cup of cheap instant coffee, spray it on the fabric, and then iron it dry. Easy!

Making the House Blocks

Sort the dark prints so that each of the House blocks is made up of a main color for the house and a second color for the side of the house. Pick a light print for the sky in each House block. Press all seam allowances in the directions indicated by the arrows.

1. Draw a diagonal line from corner to corner on the wrong side of two matching light 2½" squares. Place one marked square on one end of one black 2½" × 4½" rectangle, orienting the line as shown. Sew on the line. Trim the seam allowances to ¼". Repeat to sew, trim, and press the second square on the opposite end of the rectangle in the same manner. Make eight roof units.

Make 8 units, 2½" × 4½".

2. Make the door units for each of the eight houses by sewing a black 1½" × 2½" rectangle between each matching set of 2" × 2½" print rectangles. The door unit should measure 2½" × 4½", including the seam allowances.

Make 8 units, 2½" × 4½".

3. Draw a diagonal line from corner to corner on the wrong side of eight of the remaining light squares. Place the squares on one end of each brown, gold, and orange 2½" × 4½" rectangle with right sides together. Sew on the line, and then trim the seam allowances to ¼". Make eight side units.

Make 8 units, 2½" × 4½".

4. Lay out one door unit, one matching house 2½" × 4½" rectangle, one roof unit, one side unit, and one light 2½" square as shown. Join the pieces in each row, and then sew the rows together. The block should measure 6½" square, including the seam allowances. Repeat to make eight House blocks.

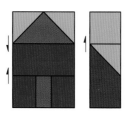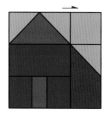

Make 8 blocks,
6½" × 6½".

Making the Embroidered Blocks

1. Transfer the embroidery patterns (page 79) to the Osnaburg squares, using a light box and water-soluble pen. Fuse the batting squares or fusible interfacing to the back of the Osnaburg squares.

2. Thread a needle with wool embroidery thread or two strands of cotton embroidery floss. Embroider the designs according to the embroidery key. For the bird's breast, fill in the area with a satin stitch or seed stitch, or select the triple stitch on your sewing machine and fill in the area by machine. You may also do all of the backstitching with the triple-stitch machine method. When sewing with wool thread in your machine, use a topstitch needle and cotton thread in the bobbin. Loosen the tension slightly.

3. After the embroidery is complete, press the blocks and trim them to 6½" square, centering the designs.

Assembling the Quilt Top

1. Lay out the blocks in five rows of three, alternating the House and embroidered blocks as shown in the quilt assembly diagram, above right. Join the blocks in each row, and then

join the rows. The quilt top should measure 18½" × 30½", including the seam allowances.

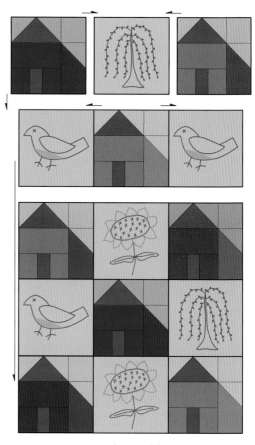

Quilt assembly

2. Sew the black 2" × 30½" strips to the sides of the quilt. Press the seam allowances toward the borders. The quilt top should measure 21½" × 30½". Sew the black 2" × 21½" strips to the top and bottom of the quilt. Press the seam allowances toward the borders. The quilt top should measure 21½" × 33½".

Finishing the Quilt

Go to ShopMartingale.com/HowtoQuilt for more details on quilting and finishing.

1. Layer the backing, batting, and quilt top; baste the layers together. Hand or machine quilt as desired. The quilt shown was machine quilted with an allover stippling design.

2. Use the brown 2½"-wide strips to make the binding and then attach it to the quilt.

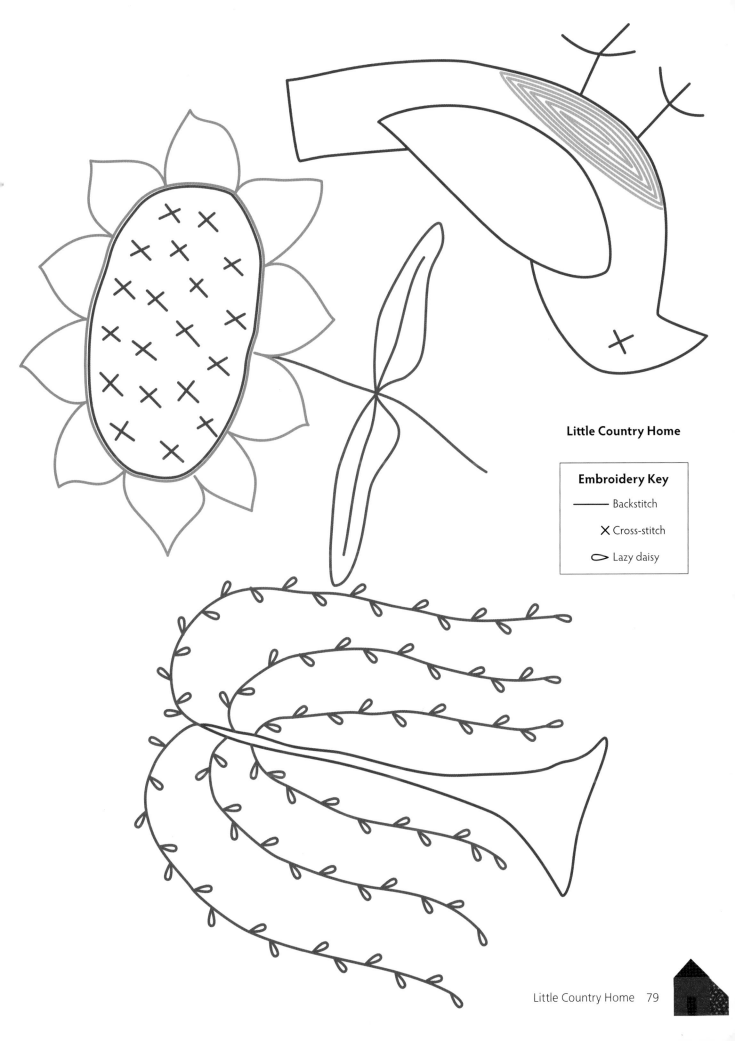

Little Country Home

Embroidery Key

—— Backstitch

✗ Cross-stitch

◯ Lazy daisy

About the Contributors

Tonya Alexander

Tonya says that she's an accidental quilter by home-decorating necessity; her first quilt was meant to be her only quilt. But a love of fabric, scraps, and stash quickly overtook her. She is the author of *Stash Lab* (Martingale, 2015). Visit Tonya at EyeCandyQuilts.blogspot.com.

Natalie Barnes

Natalie is the owner of beyond the reef, a pattern-design company, and is happy to be traveling to teach, lecture, and inspire other quilters. She is the author of *A Modern Twist* (Martingale, 2015). You can find her at beyondthereefpatterns.com.

Dana Bolyard

Dana is a wife, mother, soap maker, photographer, thrifter, blogger, and quilter. When not shuttling kids to and fro or tending her garden, she is usually at her sewing machine—or scheming to find her way there soon. Dana is the author of *Imagine Quilts* (Martingale, 2014). Visit her online at OldRedBarnCo.blogspot.com.

Melissa Corry

Melissa began quilting as a hobby in 2002 and started a blog in 2010. Her hobby has become a passion that she shares through tutorials, patterns, and her book, *Irish Chain Quilts* (Martingale, 2015). Visit her at HappyQuiltingMelissa.com.

Sherri Falls

Sherri is the owner of This & That Pattern Company. In 2000, she started a machine-quilting business with her mother, who owns a quilt store in scenic Waconia, Minnesota. Sherri is the author of *Sew This and That!* (Martingale, 2016). You can visit her at ThisandThatPatterns.com.

Jeni Gaston

Jeni has been sewing and crafting with her three sisters since she was a little girl. For 10 years, Jeni and her sister Gretchen owned and operated the Woolen Willow Quilt Shop. Jeni is the author of *Primitive Style* (Martingale, 2015). You can find her at WoolenWillowDesigns.com.

Kimberly Jolly

Kimberly owns Fat Quarter Shop, an online fabric store, and It's Sew Emma, a pattern company. Her designs are often inspired by vintage quilts and blocks, but she occasionally ventures out to try something new. She loves to create quilts for friends and family, especially her children, who are a constant source of inspiration.

Sherri McConnell

Sherri received her first sewing machine when she was about 10 years old and has been sewing clothing and home-decor items ever since. After receiving a "gentle push" from her grandmother, she branched out into quilting and hasn't stopped. Find Sherri at AQuiltingLife.com.

Carrie Nelson

A rose by any other name is still a rose. So fans of Carrie may not know her by her given name, but they surely know her by her pattern-designer name, Miss Rosie. Carrie has joined Moda Fabrics as the guru of social media, but she still slips into her Miss Rosie mode from time to time to design yet another clever scrappy pattern. No matter what you call her, you'll call her patchwork patterns brilliant! Visit her at blog.ModaFabrics.com.

Amanda Niederhauser

Amanda, aka Jedi Craft Girl, has been sewing since she was eight years old. With a passion for all things creative, she has been quilting for more than 16 years and has the stash to prove it. Amanda enjoys sharing her love for crafting, sewing, quilting, thrifting, and more. Visit her blog at JediCraftGirl.com.

Sarah Price

Known for her ability to provide beautiful quilt patterns that are easy to read and follow, Sarah is the pattern stylist for It's Sew Emma. Sarah specializes in creating clear layouts, instructions, and diagrams for an array of pretty quilts.

Christa Watson

An award-winning sit-down machine quilter, Christa designs quilt patterns and teaches workshops. She's the author of *Machine Quilting with Style* and the coauthor of *The Ultimate Guide to Machine Quilting* (Martingale, 2015 and 2016 respectively). Christa enjoys being a wife and a mom. You can find her at ChristaQuilts.com.

Jackie White

A quilt teacher, lecturer, and pattern designer, Jackie has a passion for creating three-dimensional art quilts. Her patterns have been published in several books and magazines. When Jackie isn't quilting, she's at her farm with her two boys and her husband. Find her online at JabotQuilt.blogspot.com.

Corey Yoder

A quilty mom of two girls and wife to one great husband, Corey enjoys playing with fabric in the form of quilts and quilt design. You can find her at CorianderQuilts.com.